DR. MAHINDER C. WATSA

THE SEXPERT A VISIONARY AND A PIONEER

NILAN SINGH

INDIA • SINGAPORE • MALAYSIA

ISBN 979-8-88935-829-9

For any information related to this book:
Please email – drwatsabook@gmail.com

In memory of a Legend

In fulfilment of his Dream

We made it happen Dad!

Deepa, Gautam, Ayesha & Leisha Watsa

We gratefully acknowledge all those who have helped put this biography together by sharing anecdotes; and their memories and affectionate recollections.

CONTENTS

Design: **GODWIN GONSALVES** Editorial Support: **STEPHEN REGO**

FOREWORD

Dr. Mahinder C. Watsa, our Dad, widely known as Minny, was very keen to write his autobiography. Unfortunately, he was always busy with his work and never could get down to it.

When he thought he had some time, and had just started on it, Covid broke out and lockdown was imposed suddenly. Sadly, he passed away before lockdown was lifted and he could work on this project, which was so close to his heart and his dream remained just that – a will-o'-the-wisp.

We commissioned this biography, both as a tribute to him and as going some way in fulfilling one of his greatest desires towards the end; to thus encapsulate the life, work and achievements of one of the tallest men in the field of Sexuality Education, Counselling and Therapy in the country.

Dad was a man of many dimensions and several facets: intensely and seriously dedicated to his lifework; extremely humorous, with a mischievous bent of mind; a loyal and loving family man; a reliable, rock of a friend; an able leader of people; an inspiring colleague; an enthusiastic socialiser – and a great foodie.

He was a total charmer and often told us that his friends called him "Sexy Watsa". On one of his birthdays, we hosted a small dinner party for him at a club and, as a joke, we got him a tie which said "I am sexy and I know it". Far from being embarrassed, he happily flaunted it cheerfully all evening to his friends!

When it came to sex, he maintained, Indians alternate between extremely confused and extremely obsessive. Thus, he made it his mission to rescue people from long years of sexual misinformation – or indeed lack of any scientific information. He not only took it upon himself to educate people on the subject of sex and sexuality, but also worked to see that it became part of the curriculum in schools.

In the later years of his professional life, he observed that there were many more women writing in to him; and even at seminars, a lot more women would come forward to ask questions. The general feeling amongst the female population was: "Dr. Watsa knows what women want". Moreover, even the age group of people writing to him had expanded widely and became varied – from adolescents to senior citizens.

This gave him immense satisfaction as he felt that his work over so many decades was finally paying off – he had managed to break the barrier to issues of sexuality!

Dad always said sexology may not sound as sexy as cardiology or gastroenterology but it accounts for a sizable number of problems faced by both, men and women; as well as young children and adolescents.

He often told us that in the 1980s, the newspapers would not print anything related to sex or sexology.

Whilst he received many awards for his work he also received plenty of verbal abuses and threats. He took it all in his stride, without losing his cool.

The *BBC* had featured him in a podcast, the *New York Times* had written about him, a Dutch journalist had interviewed him, as had numerous publications and other media within the country – but most of all, the youth in India idolised him.

He often told us that he deliberately used a rather terse style of writing because, "Who wants to read a tome?" He said: "I want to educate people not to bore them. One should never make sex boring."

There was a daily ritual which never allowed Dad, even at 96, to be distracted or enjoy even a brief holiday. Every morning, as soon as he woke up he would sit down at his computer. His glasses and light would go on at the same time, to find a mailbox that had filled up again between the previous night and the morning. The mails were from people who were all looking for answers from the man who had brought sex and sexuality out of the closet and put it on the table – a topic to be discussed and taught openly and in a forthright manner.

In the last few years of his life he became particularly popular for his daily column in the *Mumbai Mirror*. His witty and straightforward advice in *Ask the Sexpert* earned him – apart from an ever full inbox – a cult status reaching far beyond Mumbai. He would answer every question he received, even the most absurd; and always with a dollop of humour which he felt helped.

His humour was of the P.G. Wodehouse type, which cut across generations. Little wonder then, that he acknowledged Wodehouse as his favourite author.

Dad was an absolute workaholic, and always needed his laptop around at all times – a rare trait for a man of his age. Yet, even that reflected on just how advanced the man was in all things. He would be invariably busy reading up on the latest news, especially in the fields of science and medicine. Even whilst on a small vacation he was always eager to get back to his work and his laptop.

He was often referred to as the "Sexologist of the Century". We hope that this book goes some way in explaining this title; as well as to introduce the man that he was in totality, along with an insight into what made him tick, to all who accorded him so much respect, reverence and affection.

We hope you enjoy this offering of ours in memory of a great Visionary and a Pioneer.

Deepa & Gautam Watsa

INTRODUCTION

Dr. Mahinder Watsa, or "Minny" as we knew him, and I go back a long, long way. Our association at multiple levels has been described at various points in this book. Hence, I do not wish to repeat those details here.

Suffice it to say, that our friendship, which began in our youth, spanned more than seven decades. Moreover, Dr. Watsa and I both specialised in Obstetrics & Gynaecology. So, our paths crossed time and again, not only on the personal front, but on the professional one as well.

In a sense, I consider him to be my first teacher when I started out in my professional life. This was when he was Registrar and I was House Surgeon at Nair Hospital. The lessons I learnt from him then – including how to be calm in every situation – have stayed with me through the years.

I have only mentioned the bonds we shared at the outset to stress that I was fortunate enough to have what could be described as a 'ringside view' of Dr. Watsa's emergence as the outstanding, transformative personality that he finally became.

I thus saw, and often shared at close quarters, the varied experiences of different phases of his life. I knew the young medical student who, while focusing on his studies, also found time for sports and social life. I was in regular contact with him during his early forays into the professional world at Nair, Bhabha and Wadia hospitals where he deepened his knowledge and skills in ObGyn, and later, during his years of private practice at Bandra and his stint at Glaxo.

It was the cumulative impact of all the years of practice that led him to a more in-depth exploration of sexuality, and the next phase of his career. I was the one who introduced him to Avabai Wadia and the Family Planning Association of India (FPAI), which marked the beginning of his heyday – the work he did at FPAI, including the setting up of SCERT; and the founding of CSEPI. We continued to remain close during our later years even as he scaled a new pinnacle as the much venerated author of *Ask the Sexpert* column in *Mumbai Mirror.*

His life was akin to a pebble that when dropped into a pool of water, causes never ceasing ripples. These expanded relentlessly over the decades, often pushing past obstacles to conquer a number of unknown and till-then 'secret' frontiers. And, dare I add, the 'pebble' continues to impact the world of sexuality medicine even after his passing.

There are various manifestations of the changes in the system that resulted, directly or indirectly, from this push past old boundaries. To name a few: today, we see a wide acceptance of Sexual Medicine as a specialised field with trained practitioners; a systematic introduction of sex education at different levels for children and youth; a not insignificant number of organisations, including a few official bodies, that have focused their efforts in these, and related areas; and the ever-swelling ranks of highly trained and well-equipped professionals in different parts of the country who help guide and minister to those in need of help.

Of course, Dr. Watsa has long been known and respected by particular segments of society, each of which related to certain aspects of his life. Like me, there are many professionals involved in medicine, as well as those in sexuality-related fields who grasp the enormous value of his path-breaking efforts. There are thousands, or maybe lakhs of patients who have benefitted directly and indirectly, from his work. And there is that huge fan-following of his – the youth who had their queries answered, their doubts addressed and their fantasies and wild imagination brought down to earth through the letters he answered; a few through the public columns in the newspapers, but many more personally as well.

Till now, there was no 'larger canvas', where all these various aspects came together to provide a complete picture.

I am therefore delighted that his family has taken the initiative to publish his biography, bringing these myriad facets of my friend and colleague together in one place; and capturing the wide spectrum of things that he did and said in one easy-to-read volume.

I believe it is a fitting tribute to a man who was literally larger than life, and who achieved so much in one lifespan.

It is my ardent wish that as a result of this eminently readable book, Dr. Mahinder C. Watsa, our Minny, and his work gets introduced to people far and wide.

Dr. Rustom (Rusi) Soonawala

PREFACE

From a person whom I had barely heard of – much less known about the breadth and depth of his life's work – to becoming a voice in my head, and a fellow traveller through the writing of his biography, the Doctor and I have traversed a great distance.

At the beginning, whenever I mentioned his name, there was immediate recognition – all due to his pithy, witty, spicy *Mumbai Mirror* column, *Ask the Sexpert.* That's when I became acquainted with his cult-like popularity.

Then, as I spoke to his family, colleagues and friends; read about him and perused his writings, I discovered the man that he was in a 360-degree sense. It was like an archaeological find – you first glimpse merely a portion of it; then as you clear away the layers under which it was buried, the entire artefact is revealed in all its glory and its complete significance.

I discovered that though the youth connected with him like they did with no other living 90-plus-year-old, Dr. Mahinder C. Watsa's work and contribution did not begin and end in the last decade-and-a-half of his life; but had spanned more than the previous six decades.

As one dug deeper, one got to see his greatness for what it was: a visionary outlook and a pioneering contribution. This included taking ahead the understanding of sexuality in its full sense; and the proliferation of its education, particularly in India, with an impact also in a few countries in the region. It encompassed, too, his work of counselling and providing therapy to patients suffering from malaise rooted in this aspect, which had remained suppressed and untreated due to embarrassment and not knowing whom to go to for help.

Apart from education and treatment, there was the other major contribution: the creation of an army of scientifically trained sexologists who are today out there helping patients deal with their traumas.

Considering that Dr. Watsa's life had spanned so many decades it was difficult to envisage the times he had been born into and the eras he had lived through; the understanding of which helped in assessing and appreciating how great his contribution really is.

Also, one realised that while his latter day work – mainly the column – was known, shared, and talked about; not much was known of his earlier work except among his former colleagues and close co-workers.

Out of these two realisations was born the structure of the book – each chapter of his life is preceded by a very brief glimpse into the period we are talking about. Needless to say, this is, at best, only a very subjective and cursory reference to the times – as this is not a historical treatise, but the story of one man's life and his contribution. These brief outlines are just that: reminders of the particular time being referred to.

Similarly, I have presented short excerpts from his earlier writings and, in places, from his own book at the end of each chapter. Again, while these are in no way detailed or even necessarily related to the period of his life we are covering in that chapter, they provide a very valuable insight into just how forward thinking the man was.

He was not just ahead of his times; but his sensibilities and his sympathies were very naturally of an advanced, broad-minded outlook. His attitude to women, persons of differing sexual identities, his lack of being judgmental whatever the scenario sketched out by his patients, his ability to see the larger socio-economic roots of individual problems and his never failing gentleness and understanding made him stand out as a man like no other.

As a minor aside, I would also like to mention that through the writing of this book, I got a slight glimpse of the leading lights of the Family Planning Association of India (FPAI) and their lives and times. Their stories are compelling and transported me to a period when men and women were motivated by ideals; and were, in fact, most open to change and in adopting new ideas in their thoughts and actions.

For me, this biography represents a fascinating exploration through timescapes and thoughtscapes. I hope I have managed to share with you all something of that enchanting and extraordinary voyage.

Nilan Singh

CHAPTER 1

THE SEXPERT

2020

The year heralding the stepping of the world into the third decade of the 21st century began like any other. Some partied, some slept through the magic midnight hour. The pendulum swung in a seeming continuum between one year and the next: what had been happening on one side of the date divide continued onto the other. Just because the calendar had changed did not mean that the world had. Or so we all thought. Till later events made us realise how wrong we were.

For, in the womb of the old year pregnant with the new, also lay nestled like an evil twin, a disaster capsule waiting to make its explosive entry into the world.

2020. A year which turned the globe on its head. A year that unleashed a hurricane of sorrow, in the wake of a dreadful pandemic which had a ravaging impact on every part of the world. A time which taught us many sound lessons too. Certainly not a year to be forgotten in a hurry.

And, even as 2020 was drawing to a close, like a scorpion with a sting in its tail, the year swept away with it, a colossus. Though his was no Covid death, it was yet, a tragedy in its own way. For, here was a man who had performed some Herculean tasks – at a time when to talk frankly of sex was taboo in India, he had first started educating people, particularly adolescents, about it, convinced that this was the only way to curb the many ills related to sexual issues in society. In more recent years, he had been friend, philosopher, guide and counsellor to people of all ages ridden with sexual angst. While the term might raise a few sniggers, maybe a few embarrassed giggles, these are real problems afflicting vast numbers of the populace, particularly the young; sometimes resulting in real physical and psychological harm.

"A great man does not seek applause or place; he seeks for truth; he seeks the road to happiness, and what he ascertains, he gives to others."

Robert Green Ingersoll
American lawyer, writer and orator

Until the early part of 2020, if anyone walking on the seafront at Shivaji Park (locally known as Dadar Chowpatty) in Mumbai was to cast an upward look towards the buildings hugging the shoreline, their glance might perhaps have fallen on the tall, powerfully built figure, slightly stooping with age, looking down at the flow and ebb of the tide on the beach below; and also taking in the ever changing pattern of humanity swirling around like a kaleidoscope on the street. Here a couple turning its back on the world to create a universe of their own, there another couple in a passionate clinch; here a child pulling strenuously at her mother's hand to break free and there a group of teenagers perched on a wall laughing and joking; and there again, an elderly couple taking their daily walk. Or then, the vast multitudes, merely going about their business: men, women and children – of various ages, with varying backgrounds and with different problems and proclivities. Their inner selves, and turmoil, if any, hidden behind the veil of social correctness, socially appropriate behaviour, strictly regulated by social expectations. Who knows what lay beneath the surface? Happiness? Joy? Frustration? Hurt? Anger? All of the above or none?

Yet, all of them would be appraised with the same calm, measured glance; the same philosophically assessing demeanour. And, if anyone encountered the figure leaning on a stick and taking a walk in the open grounds of Shivaji Park, or sitting sheltered beneath one of the large *saman* trees lining its periphery, they might have cast a benign look, perhaps given a nod or a smile at the grandfatherly person.

In a moment of idle curiosity kindled by the still impressive figure; the face still echoing the handsome features of his youth upon which were overlaid the lines wrought by age and experience, some may have wondered about this elderly gentleman. What could his profession have been when he was a young man? Never in their wildest dreams could they have guessed that the gentleman was not only still active professionally, but he was that most popular persona – The Sexpert – whose column in the *Mumbai Mirror* (and its other city editions) had been all the rage for close to 15 years.

For, Dr. Mahinder C. Watsa who celebrated his 96th birthday on February 11, 2020 was indeed the man behind the caustic wit, the man who provided answers to convoluted, sometimes outré – and, frankly, quite outrageous – questions. The man, who untangled complex knots in relationships, and soothed many a fevered brow. With only the turn of a phrase – which could on occasion have the twist of a knife, if the question was flagrantly unreasonable, unscientific or just plain dim-witted – he would unfailingly point in the correct direction, spelling out a practical, scientific solution. The youth reading his column, *Ask the Sexpert* would hang on to his every word, for, he was their true North in a turbulent world awash with lack of knowledge and information about all matters sexual, and the problems arising as a result.

Anyone could be forgiven for not realising that THIS was the man who anchored THAT column. For one, the column was about a subject that was still met with sniggers, giggles and rolling of the eyes. And then, the tone in which it was written – witty, humorous and sometimes acerbic – was presumed to be that of a person much, much younger. How could this grandfatherly figure write about sex and that too, in such a with it, contemporary manner?

In a seeming contradiction, if one mentioned the word "sexologist" to people – across generations – in an almost Pavlovian response, many would say "Oh Dr. Watsa!" Such was the power of the brand that he had so effortlessly become.

In fact, among the youth, he held the stature of an icon bringing to mind the era of pop stars and their fans, incongruous as it may seem. Reminiscent of the kind of frenzy that seized groupies and camp followers in yester years, several WhatsApp groups mushroomed which would share and comment on 'Watsaisms'; memes did the rounds; fans tweeted regularly about this or that question – sometimes adding their own, witty comments; and lists were compiled of "The Best of Dr. Watsa" – not just by newspapers and magazines, but even by his admirers, which segment included film stars, film makers, and comedians amongst a host of others. Social media was pulsating with the wisdom of Watsa, in the last decade and more.

Dr. Watsa's popularity was also evident in the 2017 released documentary film about him directed and produced by Vaishali Sinha, titled – you guessed it – *Ask the Sexpert.*

In one of the scenes, a couple of young men are asked about the column. One of them replies with an embarrassed but enthusiastic grin remembering even the page number the column would regularly appear on, while admitting "Yeah. Everyone knows it."

Many others interviewed in the film go on to frankly express appreciation of the column which helped them voice their innermost secret worries and clarify many misconceptions about sex.

One avowed admirer is the successful stand-up comedian Aditi Mittal. Amongst her most popular characterisations, Dr. Mrs. Lutchuke (though a woman) is based loosely on Dr. Watsa's character with a similar passion for sex education.

When Dr. Watsa happened to attend one of her shows, she had an ecstatic reaction, later shared on Twitter with several "OMGs" thrown in.

In *Ask the Sexpert* she exclaims, "And when he came for the show I was just flipping out!"

"There is something very non-threatening about an older person speaking about sex," Aditi adds reflectively. "That is what Mahinder Watsa has going for him." More importantly, she salutes him when she says: "The way he spoke, made it possible for me to speak more freely."

Dr. Watsa's former colleague and longtime friend Dr. Saroj Jha, who had accompanied him to the show has vivid memories of how enthusiastically the audience reacted to his presence. "People were screaming because they recognised him, and he was mentioned in the show as well! There was a crowd of people waiting to be photographed with him," she enthuses.

This scenario was to be re-enacted again and again whenever Dr. Watsa had occasion to make a public appearance after he was identified as 'The Sexpert' through the film and other media coverage.

Vaishali herself has many fond memories of the time she was shooting with the iconic Dr. Watsa. "I saw how he always loved to start his speeches with a joke," she says, narrating a favourite anecdote. "I remember one such event. He opened his speech at the 30th National Conference of Sexology in Mumbai saying: 'Respected dignitaries, I have attended many conferences, and this has made me many sincere friends. Some of my friends even pray for me, and they say, 'Please, God, put your arms around his shoulders but put your hand over his mouth!'" Such was his humour which took everyone along, especially since he was even able to laugh at himself with utter confidence.

Vaishali's film *Ask the Sexpert* became a huge hit on the film festival circuit; and was invited to over 60 festivals held all over the world.

She adds: "In India, it was my great pleasure to have him accompany me at the film's premiere during the MAMI festival in Mumbai; where he received a standing ovation from his home crowd."

Another person who had worked with him, Armin Jamshedji, former

Director Monitoring & Evaluation at the FPAI, recalls how she was present on two occasions at the theatre screenings during the Mumbai Film Festival in 2017. "I was completely amazed to see huge crowds of people waiting to see him – like he was a star!" she says with incredulity writ large in her words.

In fact, in the course of the film, Dr. Watsa is asked by the filmmaker, "Do you find your popularity surprising?"

In his characteristic understated style, he replied with a chuckle "Yes definitely. We did this for 40 years and no one even bothered. And suddenly in the 41st year, somebody is bothering." Translation: Dr. Watsa had been a sex education warrior for decades. He had been relentlessly working at pulling sex out of the closet, in a manner of speaking, and putting it on the table for frank dialogue about it. But it was only in the past dozen years or so (at the time of the film's making), that a wider section of people began sitting up and taking notice. What is more, they were actually appreciating the work he was doing; something which he had been pursuing almost as a crusade – not for the sake of gratification of any kind, but as a matter of conviction about its necessity, in order to promote the general health and welfare of society.

In a BBC World Service podcast *My Indian Life* – "It's all about being young and being Indian in the 21st century" – anchor Kalki Koechlin once featured Dr. Watsa. At the outset of the Episode, Kalki explained that though the show generally highlighted the stories of young people, Dr. Watsa, despite the fact he was 94 years old (at the time), "had a youthfulness about him". More importantly, she stressed, it was his "massive, massive" popularity with the youth which made him an extremely attractive proposition for the show. In the course of the podcast, he is described as "cool, sassy, witty and progressive".

A young student summed it up when she said that some might think that Dr. Watsa is in his 30s or 40s, going by his column. But, she said, considering that he is 90 plus (his writing) "is just out of this world".

If there was one programme which highlighted just how iconic he had become, it was the particularly cleverly put together promotion of the hit film *Badhai Ho* around its release date in 2018. The film was about a senior woman, mother of a grown up son, getting pregnant; and the resultant hue and cry amongst the immediate family and the neighbourhood. The film starred popular actor Ayushmann Khurrana, who himself had become something of a rage amongst the youth.

The TV "show" was built around a scenario: Ayushmann (playing Nakul Kaushik) and his girlfriend in the film, actress Sanya Malhotra (playing Renee Sharma), visit Dr. Mahinder Watsa for a consultation as the young man is very disturbed that his mother has conceived at this late age. He is traumatised both at the thought that his parents still have sex; as well as the fact that she is pregnant and the target of all the gossip. The show itself was facilitated by the Family Planning Association of India (FPAI), an organisation that Dr. Watsa had been an intrinsic part of in the past (more about that later). The promotional show had a certain wackiness about it – maintaining as it did the fiction of the film's characters in interaction with the very real sexologist who counselled them – even presenting them with his book *It's Normal,* which seemed to be underlining his reassurance to Ayushmann.

Sagarika Choudhary writing in (the online version of) *Mumbai Mirror* updated on December 29, 2020 – the day after the legend passed away – said: "Dr. Watsa even inspired Boman Irani's character of the sexologist Dr. Vardhi in the film *Made in China.* In fact, the director of the film, Mikhil Musale had actually paid several visits to the sexpert's office to develop Boman's character, and later termed him as one of the most 'honest and experienced' human beings he has met."

Inspiring the performing arts was not something new: Dr. Suchitra Dalvie, also an erstwhile colleague who remained in touch till the end, recalls seeing a play some 10-15 years back which actually featured his character. Though the name of the play and other details of the production are lost in the mists of time, Dr. Dalvie does remember the storyline. "It was about a Parsi couple whose daughter returns from abroad with a live-in partner," she narrates. "The parents don't know how to deal with it – they are in a dilemma about how they should respond. The play actually had a Dr. Watsa character and the couple consult him. And just like in his columns, his character was portrayed as being very broadminded – he tells the parents words to the effect that as the young couple are consenting adults, they should be allowed to make their own decisions about how they want to live their life."

A few years ago, Dr. Watsa already in his 90s, received a letter from an 18-year old girl. Echoing the views of the girl on Kalki's show, she says she was stunned when she realised how old Dr. Watsa was – she had thought he was in his 40s until she saw a picture of him. And one can almost hear her wail when she writes, "What will happen when you are no more there? Your column is a life-saving experience for us. Millions of people depend on your advice. We all love you, Dr. Mahinder Watsa."

That's how ubiquitous the man's popularity was. As he rode the crest of his fame, you could love him (as most did) or hate him (as few did) – but you just could not ignore the phenomenon that was Dr. Mahinder C. Watsa.

Rewind to over 15 years back. It was the year 2005. Meenal Baghel, the talented and feisty former editor of the hugely successful *Mumbai Mirror* – a publication of Bennett, Coleman & Co. Ltd. and sister publication of India's leading newspaper *The Times of India* – was trying to fit in the final jigsaw pieces to her dummy of the soon to be launched daily tabloid. She had a good idea of what the front pages of the paper and the back pages of the paper would contain – what sort of city, political, sports and other stories she would like to include. But she was still searching for something more to add, a special hook – something that would have intrinsic appeal to readers.

That was when she recalled an Agony Aunt column anchored by a designer socialite in one of newspapers she had formerly worked with. She remembered the number of letters it had attracted, and the genuine cry for help that emanated from most of them.

Yet, one letter and the response to it remained embedded in her mind like a particularly prickly thorn. A Class 10 boy who was due to appear for his Board exams had written in to say that he couldn't focus on his studies as he was in the habit of masturbating; and he was feeling very disturbed about it. The advice that the person answering gave was something to the effect that his behaviour would invite "bad karma". Needless to say, it was a very negative way to tackle the situation, and in all probability must have further 'disturbed' the hapless kid.

"Even in those days we got a lot of letters relating to sexual problems – but the Indian media was very shy of anything sexually explicit," says Meenal looking back a couple of decades. "So, when I thought of starting a column to answer questions on sexual problems, I was sure that we would not asterisk words like breasts or pubic hair or whatever. I wanted it to be a matter-of-fact, scientific column."

She and her team began the hunt for a suitable sexologist to anchor the segment. "I was very clear about the kind of column I wanted and who I didn't want to anchor it," Meenal emphasises. But that still begged the question "Then who?"

Fast forward a few days. Meenal is sitting with colleagues and they are once again discussing possibilities, when Dr. Watsa's name crops up at the top of the list. "I had not even heard of him then," she says. "But he was highly recommended. So, I called him up and had a short conversation which must have lasted all of two minutes." That brief talk resulted in Dr. Watsa readily agreeing to the assignment; and Meenal being convinced that she had found the right man for the job.

That, arguably, must be the most decisive and far-reaching two minutes in both their lives. The paper had found a sexologist for whom its young readers fell hook, line and sinker; and the good doctor with a mission had found his (new) flock – albeit that was a scenario yet to unfold.

Dr. Watsa's column made an appearance in the *Mumbai Mirror* from Day 1. Soon, there was mail literally pouring in. Maybe it was the policy that no names would be revealed that helped and was a "freeing experience", as people could express their problems openly without fear of being identified, or censured.

"Soon, there were stacks and stacks of letters," Meenal recollects with amusement. "I recall the person who used to handle the Watsa letters sitting surrounded literally by pillars of letters!"

However, all was not well in Paradise. Though the overwhelming majority took to the column immediately, there were disgruntled voices too. "You are corrupting our children" seemed to be the accusatory crux of the sentiment. The detractors also said: "There is no Dr. Watsa – you are making all this up."

"So, then, we decided to run his picture," says Meenal. "That was the first time I realised how old he was. We ran his photo for some time and carried on publishing the column, ignoring the complaints."

Her position on the matter was more than vindicated when, about six-seven months after the paper had started, the well-known psychiatrist Dr. Harish Shetty called Meenal and said that his patients said they had benefitted from Dr. Watsa's advice – which was a huge compliment. And if she needed any further affirmation of the success of the column, there was the adulation from readers that just kept snowballing.

At some point of time, a lady crusading against his column and its outspoken ways filed a case against the paper and Dr. Watsa. "We got caught up in litigation in several courts in different areas of the city. But it also gave me a chance to get to know him," says Meenal.

In an article profiling him, published in the (by now online version of) *Mumbai Mirror* on the day after Dr. Watsa's passing, Meenal shared some delightful insights into both the character of the man as well as their interaction. She wrote:

"On a certain day a few years ago when we were being harassed by an odious woman with frivolous litigation, Dr. Mahinder Watsa, then in his late 80s, and I had a particularly trying morning at the Kurla magistrate's court where we awaited our fate on a bench infested with bed bugs. As we returned to the office, the stress of the day took its toll and his knee jammed, temporarily paralysing his lower leg. Tottering on impractical heels, I rushed forward to stop him from falling, only to go flying flat on all fours with him.

"The day's ignominy was complete.

"As consolation for my failed chivalric attempt, Dr. Watsa sent me a colourful silk scarf that evening. It was also his way of suggesting how a nice gesture and a dash of jauntiness can go a long way in making an unpleasant day better. Not unlike the advice he dispenses on the pages of this newspaper. For 15 years without fail – seven days a week, 52 weeks of the year – Mahinder Watsa has responded to the tortured queries of thousands of readers with patience – endless, endless amounts of it – and with clarity, humanity and wit. (To an anguished teenager's query whether repeated masturbation will reduce the size of his organ, Dr. Watsa's bracing response: You talk every day, has your tongue become smaller?)

"Many of these questions and answers from the column that has now acquired cult status can be found in Dr. Watsa's first ever book, an essential read, called *It's Normal!* He was contemplating writing his memoirs next."

There was something very exceptional about the man. Looking back, Meenal sums it up saying: "He was paternalistic but so very funny, with a wicked sense of humour. The trouble he took to answer the questions, his great humanity, his great literary style – all of it was what made the column special."

She adds with a chuckle: "Sometimes, looking at some of the questions that people sent, I thought they were testing him, trying to match wits with him – just to see how he would respond. His was a very deadpan humour – he never put down people. That has something to do with his old-worldliness – all the courtesies were an intrinsic part of him. He would be horrified, I think, to even think of being rude to anyone!"

This is borne out by Trishla Jain, former Assistant to Dr. Watsa. She says he would regularly get a few nasty letters or hate mail too, along with the questions by eager advice seekers and fan mail.

"He would reply to each and every one of them," she recalls. "And each letter would begin with a 'Thank you'. 'Thank you for your mail', he would write, and then go on to explain his point of view in a very calm and measured manner."

For Meenal, who, till his passing on December 28, 2020, had not had much opportunity to get closely acquainted with Dr. Watsa's illustrious career before he began writing the column, what followed was an eye opener. Till then, she had believed that it was *Mumbai Mirror* which was the contributory factor to Dr. Watsa's popularity.

"The Zoom condolence meeting which was held after his passing was a truly humbling experience," she says quietly. "That was when I realised the kind of huge impact he had had on people's lives – in a sense *Mumbai Mirror* was only an incidental amplifier of his voice. At another level, I also like to think that *Mumbai Mirror* gave him a second wind. And I find it very moving, very poetic that he died a couple of weeks after *Mirror* ceased to exist in its original form."

That one observation contains within it, the microcosm of all that Dr. Watsa was, stood for, strived for and achieved. For, his life's mission and work began much, much before he became The Sexpert. It was a long road traversing the desert of ignorance, prejudice, and debilitating backward social norms. But in the course of his travels across the arid sands, he had planted some seeds of knowledge, opened some wells of hope and created some oases along the way. It was here that weary trekkers in search of clarity on sexual problems had found relief and succour; strength and solace.

Just how deep and widespread his influence was, was only realised, even by his family, after his passing. "The kind of messages that poured in and their sheer number took us by complete surprise, even though we had known how famous he was," says Gautam, Dr. Watsa's son. "Condolences were received, not just from across the country, but from all over the world too."

When one thinks about it, it's only natural, in a sense. For, Dr. Mahinder C. Watsa had worked relentlessly for over six decades to help thousands and thousands of people who faced very real problems: from anxiety about physical traits and performance to agonising about their sexual identity and how to "come out"; from failure to consummate a marriage due to lack of knowledge to inability to relate to the partner due to a variety of issues; from changes in sexual prowess and libido wrought by age to trauma caused by rape, incest, or domestic violence; and a host of other serious issues which deeply affected the well-being of adolescents and adults alike.

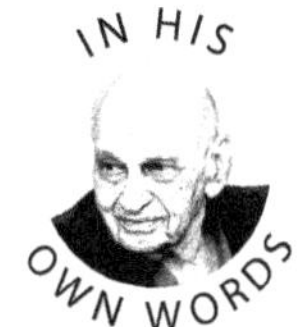

WIT & WISDOM

Some gems of wisdom from Dr. Watsa's column which were carried in the Mumbai Mirror *updated Jan 8, 2021 as a tribute to him under the head "Best responses by sexpert Dr. Watsa".*

Q *I've heard that a lizard's tail grows back when cut. I was curious if the same holds true for my penis?*

A I would advise you not to attempt such an experiment. Your penis is not a tail, and I am sure there will be no volunteers for your research.

Q *My friend feels that her breasts are getting larger because of masturbation. Is this possible?*

A No. Does she think that her clitoris is an air pump?

Q *I have a small penis and I can't seem to satisfy my girlfriend. My astrologer has advised me to pull it every day for 15 minutes while reciting a* shloka. *I have been doing this for a month but it hasn't helped. What should I do?*

A If he was right most men would have a penis hitting their knees. God doesn't help gullible foolish men. Go visit a sexpert instead who can teach you the art of making love.

Q *I've heard acidic substances can prevent pregnancy. Can I pour a few drops of lemon or orange juice into my girlfriend's vagina after intercourse?*

A Are you a bhel-puri vendor? Where did you get this weird idea? Why not try safe and easy methods like a condom instead?

Q *I am 18 years old and my testicles are larger than those I see in films. Should I be wearing a supporter all day long?*

A Do you watch movies with a ruler in one hand? Then why not measure ears and other parts of the body as well. If you have any doubt, see your doctor.

Q *I am 16-and-a-half years old, and my penis is 4.3 inches long, 1.5 inch thick (when erect). When not, it shrinks to 1 inch in thickness. I have not grown a beard yet or developed muscles. I have experienced weight loss recently too. Am I developing signs of puberty? Why is my penis short?*

A Stop sounding like a tailor. Leave your genitals alone and focus on daily exercise and a healthy diet. The genitals will look after themselves. You are already in your puberty years.

Q *If a man and a woman masturbate at the same time thinking about sex, can it lead to pregnancy?*

A There are no angels to carry your sperms to the person you are dreaming about. Fantasy gives you enjoyment but does nothing more.

CHAPTER 2

THE ECOSYSTEM OF THE ERA

1920-2020

A century, an era. Encompassing little more than a single lifetime of most people, it chronicles the narratives of millions of lives. Small bubbles of the daily existence of thousands cohere and coalesce to become buzzing beehives of society; the building blocks of history. In the course of a hundred years, events unfold, changes occur: some transformative, some incidental. How many yank out the roots of the old growth so that a completely new ecosystem can take seed and flourish? Not many, experience tells us; and certainly not those occurring over short bursts of time. This is particularly true when it comes to age-old beliefs, and centuries-held traditions. Those take time to evolve and transform into something comprehensively new.

In the meanwhile, there is constant movement in history. Sometimes as a spiral, sometimes, as a circle. In some periods, the old and new co-exist; and in others the two may even flip places.

India has witnessed much change over the last century; but much has also remained the same. Especially with regard to sex, sexuality and the attitude of society to all matters of a sexual nature. For long, they remained taboo topics where polite society was concerned. These aspects have been slow to transform in the course of natural evolution; that has needed conscious and conscientious intervention.

A large portion of the problem stemmed from the fact that society was not 'taught' to have a matter-of-fact approach to sex and sexuality. Rather, due to a variety of factors, it had been conditioned to believe that sex is dirty, and that all interaction – especially of an intimate nature – between opposite sexes (and between the same sexes, if that is their sexual orientation) is to be decried. Except, many believed, when a man and a woman are bound together by marriage.

Looked at from another angle, much had also changed over the millennia in India. Here, in certain periods since ancient times, sexuality was very much part of the discourse; and there were eras which witnessed a fairly liberal, open approach to sex. Spans of time when sex was seen as 'normal', just another facet of the fount of the pleasures of life that both men and women were free to imbibe from.

"Culture does not make people. People make culture. If it is true that the full humanity of women is not our culture, then we can and must make it our culture."

Chimamanda Ngozi Adichie
Writer

Dr. Mahinder Watsa who passed away just a few weeks before his 97th birthday, was amongst the few whose life arced over almost an entire century.

In the span straddled by those 100 years, much change was wrought worldwide and in India. The obvious, visible transformation was of course based on technological developments and innovations which have played an increasingly important role in recent decades.

The one area that had been slow to change in a fundamental manner was the social sphere – particularly in the area of gender equations, attitudes to sexuality, sexual identity; and social norms, traditions and values pertaining to these, amongst others.

Prior to the advent of the internet in the 1990s – and in India, for much of the populace even much after that – information, education, communication was only available in the traditional ways. And that is where Dr. Watsa and his team had a very important role to play.

"Sexual medicine was not recognised or offered as a subject by any University in India and is still not recognised," affirms Dr. Narayana Reddy, himself a consultant in sexual medicine and a qualified sex therapist based in Chennai; who was closely associated with Dr. Watsa over a long period of time. "Youngsters today are looking for a diploma or degree, but have no such University courses available to them."

Dr. Reddy himself is a Certified Sex Therapist (Diplomate of Sex

Therapy) and Certified Supervisor of Sex Therapy, having received his certifications from the American Association of Sexuality Educators, Counselors and Therapists (AASECT); after completing his MBBS and having received a PhD in endocrinology, for which he conducted research in herbal medicines reported to help in resolving sexual issues.

Today, apart from courses run by foreign bodies like AASECT and others, there are a few home-grown courses in sexual medicine and sexology, which are open to those who have done their MBBS or have similar degrees.

However, one of the early movers in this area was Dr. Watsa, who ran courses through various organisations and bodies he was associated with; as well as through his own Distance Education courses under the banner of Medikon Sexual Sciences.

"Dr. Watsa played a pathbreaking role in the area of sexuality education and medicine," says Dr. Rajshekhar (Raj) Brahmbhatt, amongst the leading sexologists of the day in the country, and someone who worked closely with Dr. Watsa over several decades. It was Dr. Watsa's efforts, he says, which have created an entire platoon of medical workers in the field.

For a long time in India, there were no specialist doctors to deal with issues of sexuality. Most doctors will tell you, such matters were then, and often even now are, first brought up with a family physician or general practitioner (GP); or a gynaecologist.

Today, of course, there is the field of andrology, which deals with the physical aspects of sexual issues faced by men. Sometimes, patients are sent to andrologists by family physicians to rule out physical-medical issues. If the andrologist assesses that the issue is not of a physical nature, then he will refer patients to a sexologist for counselling or therapy.

One of the foremost – and arguably, amongst the earliest – andrologists of the day, Dr. Rupin Shah, who began his medical journey in the 1970s-80s period, recalls how even in those days sex was quite a taboo subject. "Most people went to quacks rather than consult a doctor," he says ruefully.

Though he was already a doctor and had specialised in urology; he remembers that prior to setting up as an andrologist, he himself had attended workshops in sexual medicine organised by Dr. Watsa through the Council of Sex Education and Parenthood (International) more popularly known as CSEPI. Dr. Shah feels that at the time he started out, andrology was a fairly little-known area of medicine. The CSEPI workshops that he attended provided him with an overall idea of sexual medicine, counselling, and therapy; all of which have been of great use in his practice.

In the old days, it was a common sight to see large, bearded men with turbans and whiskers dressed in some tribal-looking robes, sitting on pavements with their wares of obscure origin and mysterious properties spread out in front of them – all kinds of vials, bottles, strings, beads, copper and brass rings; and claws and teeth of animals. Embarrassed men would sidle up to them and hold whispered consultations – on the roads – about their problems. And they would be given potions or some other panacea which was supposed to help them recover or preserve their powers of manhood.

These were the quacks of yesteryear; today's quacks may not sit on roads – at least not so brazenly as they did in the past – but their advertisements pop out at the unwary sufferer from various places, including from the interiors and exteriors of public transport.

Fortunately, there is today, the option of scientific treatment by scientifically trained practitioners available to patients with sexual issues.

Dr. Shirish Malde, a sexologist who was first trained in the field by Dr. Watsa and went on to work with him in the Family Planning Association of India (FPAI) set up his sexology practice in 1999 after he passed out from medical college in 1997, having specialised in urology.

Dr. Malde recalls that in his last year of medical college, he encountered more and more patients who wanted advice on such issues. He notes that particularly patients who come to Government affiliated hospitals, are invariably from the most economically deprived sections of society and do not have anyone to take their problems to.

Even in other strata of society there is a lot of hesitancy where such matters are concerned. Sometimes, it would take people years to approach doctors. "We had a situation in which even software engineers were falling prey to quacks; and the most learned men were also going to such practitioners," he says.

Dr. Malde feels that this was broadly the situation until two decades ago; and is to some extent prevalent even today.

"Someone who faces or develops a sexual problem cannot confide in their family," he observes. "People are not ready to believe that it can be a medical condition."

We are a society which doesn't talk about sex in a healthy manner, he points out. There are many sly jokes; and 90% of abusive '*gaalis*' are related to sex – mother-sister curses with sexual connotations making a mockery of women, as well as those precious relationships. It is also a travesty of our age-old value system of deifying women. Yet, the matter-of-fact mention of sex, sex education or the possibility of people encountering sexual problems is sniggered at, or shut or shot down.

"In India, there are so many myths about sex and sexuality; the word itself was taboo," bemoans Malathi Pillai, one-time colleague of Dr. Watsa at the FPAI. "So, if you said anything about it, you were looked at askance. But it's a most natural phenomenon – it's about life, how you deal with life." Malathi went on to spread her wings – encouraged by Dr. Watsa – and worked with UNICEF, doing commendable work in Africa with children, taking all that she had learned from him to further shores.

Another co-worker, who was to also remain a lifelong friend, Dr. Indira Kapoor, had earned a Diploma from the Masters & Johnson Institute in St. Louis in the USA, on a Fellowship from WHO, before she joined the FPAI. She observes: "Sexology as a topic was not covered or taught in any university – it was all kept under wraps. It was in 1990 that the turnaround started on these matters through the Government of India."

When it comes to the narrow outlook of Indian society towards sexuality the common cry of outrage against such a perspective is: "But this is the land of the *Kamasutra*!" or words to that effect.

Dr. Watsa had occasion to use the exclamation many, many times, as his associates aver – maybe in different words and quite probably in varying intonations over all the years that he practised medicine, worked in various capacities with the FPAI, set up a practice as a sexologist, counselled patients, conducted workshops, delivered lectures, consulted with and took up various activities with international organisations.

Sexuality, sexology, sexual health is not about narrow penis and vagina issues; it concerns, and is often predicated on, much wider concerns – the status of women, development of society and social health itself.

If there was one person who understood this, it was Dr. Mahinder C. Watsa. Throughout his career he was to focus on this intersection of medicine and social welfare.

"He would always say to me: 'Don't do only medical work, do socio-medical work – medicine is not an isolated thing'," remembers Dr. Dalvie. "'Even in Family Planning there are social factors at play – always look at the social angle', he would exhort."

Dr. Kalpana Apte, the current Secretary General of the FPAI, an admirer of Dr. Watsa, with whom she has interacted in the past narrates her own experience to emphasise this connect.

In the early days when she was just starting out, a young boy of perhaps 11-12 years was brought to the OPD. Upon examination she found a cauliflower type of growth in his anal region. Her mind was full of ways and means of treating the boy. Would he respond to antibiotics, should she give him penicillin, or maybe he might even require surgery? At that point she says, her mind did not for a moment think "How did he get this growth?"

The supervising senior doctor, Dr. S. I. Nagral, to whom she went to report her dilemma and get some advice on the treatment, on hearing the details just went livid. First thing he asked was "Who has come with the boy?" He summoned the man and really lambasted the guy. For, it was evident that the child was suffering from a sexually transmitted disease (STD) as a result of being sexually abused. It turned out that the person who had brought the boy to the hospital was the very person who had been abusing him. Dr. Nagral insisted that the parents be brought in and the matter be explained to them. And it was he personally operated upon the boy and took care of his treatment.

"When I look back, I see that there are so many such cases that have come up – not only sexual abuse but also domestic abuse of women," says Dr. Apte today. "Very often, even in her dying declaration, the woman is not willing to name her husband as the person responsible for her death. For, she is heartbreakingly aware that the welfare of her children will be dependent upon him, once she is no more."

Dr. Watsa always emphasised that doctors need to understand social issues and he specially stressed that any medicine is entrenched and embedded in a social context.

Armin Jamshedji shares an interesting insight. She recounts one particular project during which Dr. Watsa and his team were imparting sexuality education to youth living in slums. In the course of the workshop, the technique of 'body mapping' was used as an ice-breaker and in order to acknowledge the presence of sex organs in our body.

"I was a part of an evaluation team for this project," she says. "In the course of the workshop, the dire need for sexuality education became increasingly apparent."

The point was bought home especially when the initial ignorance of the young girls about sexual matters was revealed; and gradually, as they developed more trust and confidence, they narrated their stories of sexual abuse, and even incest. The workshops were conducted in various cities – from Bombay, to Patna, to New Delhi, to Lucknow, and to Chennai – what was revealing was that the experiences of the youngsters were similar everywhere.

Armin also recalls that even as recently as in the 21st century, health conferences focussed on social challenges like child sex abuse, child labour, child trafficking of the very young adolescents; and the need for meeting challenges through the public health approach taking into consideration the vital component of mental health.

"Dr. Watsa was a great proponent of women's rights and emphasised the underlying issue of violence against women by holding a number of seminars," she stresses.

Clearly, it was the welfare and health of people – mainly women and children – that fired Dr. Watsa's dedication and mission from the outset. This deep-rooted belief that medical issues could not be separated from social ones and the environment in which they were bred was to be an important focus and a recurrent theme in his work till the very end. It would seem – at least to some extent – he also sought out colleagues and juniors who would not only understand the connection but also be able to do something about it, due to their particular qualifications, expertise and/or areas of work.

Dr. Jha remembers how she first really bonded with him over the common ground of community medicine, though she had been acquainted with him earlier. She had attained a Diploma in Public Health and Community Medicine from the UK and returned to India. Here, she was involved in working on community health issues in slums.

"He was interested in our work in slums with Municipal drainage workers – it was part of family medicine – there was a high incidence of TB, smallpox and there was a lot of medical work needed to be done amongst them," recounts Dr. Jha.

That work also included providing sex education to the people, particularly adolescents, so that they would not fall prey to predators.

Dr. Reddy deplores the general reaction that sexology and sexologists evoke amongst the common man. After explaining the importance of a science-based practice of sexuality medicine and sex counselling he points out that even today there are many who can take patients for a ride. "There were, and still are, so many quacks who advertise promising this, that and the other. We, as serious doctors and counsellors cannot advertise," he says, referring to the medical code of conduct and ethics which prohibits qualified medical practitioners from advertising.

Dr. Reddy states emphatically: "We sexologists mean business, we are not voyeurs."

This is a realisation which is increasingly dawning on wider sections of people. Today, there are many sexologists who have set up practice across the country. The other side to the growth of this practice, an essential, is of course the fact that there are people who are willing to come out and approach doctors/sexologists and to air their concerns and problems.

Much of the credit for setting the ball in motion in order to reach this position goes to Dr. Mahinder Watsa – for putting sexology on the table and establishing its practice as a serious, scientific and essential aspect of medicine. It was he who worked relentlessly and in the face of censure and criticism to establish sex education not only for people across segments and ages, particularly adolescents; but also for doctors and medical professionals, who were often clueless as to how to deal with the issues they were confronted with.

"Everything he did was remarkable," sums up Dr. Dalvie. "He was a visionary."

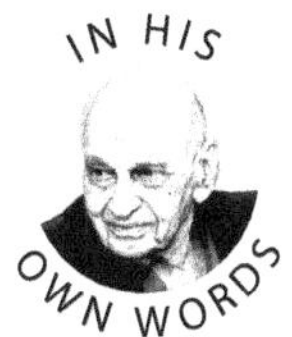

STARTING OUT ON Q&A

Dr. Mahinder C. Watsa had got down to the business of providing answers to troubling questions about sex and sexuality, particularly to adolescents and teenagers, several decades prior to the launch of the Mumbai Mirror *column* Ask the Sexpert. *The earliest extant collection of his question-and-answer wisdom is the booklet he had prepared exactly thirty years before he started writing the column for Mumbai Mirror. That was when he was Consultant and Head, SECRT Family Life & Marriage Counselling Centres of the Family Planning Association of India. What is noteworthy is the spectrum and range of topics he covers, and that, in the most matter-of-fact manner.*

Reproduced below are excerpts in the form of a few questions and answers from the booklet; and a Foreword by Dr. Watsa.

Teenagers Ask
The Doctor Answers

A publication of the Family Planning Association of India (First Edition: 1975)

Foreword

Entering adolescence can be bewildering. Attitudes of parents seem to change overnight; the behaviour of people can be very puzzling, while unexplained emotional disturbances are frequent and confusing.

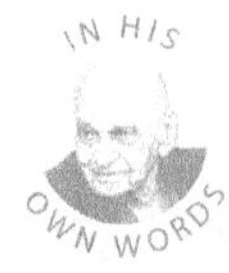

All boys and girls as they mature must go through this phase and its effects to a lesser or a greater extent.

This brief question-and-answer booklet is an attempt to deal with some of the problems commonly encountered by the young. By no means complete, we hope it will prove useful to parents as it provides answers to the many questions that growing children ask and to teenagers, as it clears many points that trouble them.

If you feel you have a question or a problem you feel you cannot discuss with your parents or family doctor, write in confidence to:

The Consultant FPAI-SECRT, Family Life & Marriage Counselling Centre.

Q *You talk of puberty – what does it mean? What really happens?*

A Adolescence is usually defined as the period in a boy's or girl's life which occurs between childhood and adulthood. Adolescence begins with puberty, which technically is a time when your secondary sex characteristics appear.

On an average, a child enters a period of accelerated growth just prior to pubescence. The greatest increase in height occurs around 11½ years of age for girls and around 14 years for boys. The sexual organs both of the male and female grow to adulthood at this stage. Girls usually start their first menstrual period between 11 and 14 year of age. Other signs like the filling out of the body, enlargement of the breasts, growth of hair under the arms and pubis for girls; change of voice, increase in size of genitalia and growth of hair in the groins for boys, also occur around 11 to 15 years of age and complete themselves by 14 years for girls and 15 years for boys on an average. Medically, a boy or girl is now capable of intercourse and can actually procreate i.e. have a baby.

Puberty is often considered a period of storm and stress as the child suddenly develops a sex drive, experiences a widening horizon, and enters a life which is not cut and dried and decided for him. These factors generate anxiety or emotional stress and may often provoke defensive behaviour which may, in extreme cases, lead to delinquency (a striking out against society) or, more commonly, result in conflict or belligerence towards adult authority, e.g., against parents and teachers. Day-dreaming, which may be construed as a means through which gratification of frustrated needs is achieved increases during this period of life. During this difficult stage the need to have people around you, who understand this is normal behaviour is imperative. You may approach your parents, teachers, priests, elder brothers and sisters, but it is important that there be understanding on both sides, and you, the teenager, must also try and appreciate the difficulties which adults experience in understanding you.

Q *I am 16 and I feel depressed and moody and want to keep to myself. Is this normal?*

A Whether you are male or female, this is a period when your moods will change rapidly. Have you noticed that there are times when you are bubbling with laughter or are on the verge of tears without any apparent cause to provoke these mood variations? Because of the rapid changes within your body and the consequent emotional

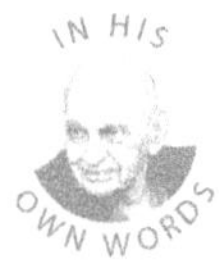

reaction, you have a natural inclination to withdraw from all problems and therefore from others. This is where your innate urge to seek human company can help you greatly. You must will yourself to take part in the social activities of your school or college, such as dramatics, and health activities like swimming, athletics, etc. There will be a strong natural desire to read love stories and erotic books. Though there is no particular harm in this, to do so exclusively tends to make escapism attractive, reduces the will to face your daily problems and limits your mental horizon.

Q *My voice breaks, my friends tease me about the hair on my chin and what is most embarrassing is that I get erections when I see a girl in a swimming costume. I am feeling desperate. What shall I do? I feel a lot of things have gone wrong with me.*

A The reason for the breaking of your voice and the other changes mentioned has already been explained earlier, and is a result of puberty. The stiffening of the penis or erection is quite natural at your age.

When a person is excited sexually, extra blood flows into the penis, causing it to become stiff. It is true that male babies and young boys have erections for reasons other than sex, but in adolescents and adults, it is normally due to sexual excitement; nevertheless, even until quite late in life, a man may wake up in the morning with an erection for no reason at all. These are natural happenings and beyond your control. The occurrence varies from person to person and is as normal as being tall or short. The variations are due to a person's attitudes and interest in sex. You can thus see that there is no need to worry or to consider your involuntary reactions as being abnormal.

Since it is desirable to sublimate sexual energy till such time as you can marry, it would do you a lot of good to indulge in healthy outdoor games, group discussions and community activity, where boys and girls work together for a good cause. Developing the right attitude towards girls is important, as this will reflect in your behaviour.

My breasts are small and flat and I look more like a boy. How can I develop a good bust?

A It is very unfortunate that the mass media has created such a fetish about the female breast which is primarily meant to suckle the new-born infant.

The breast is made up of glands and fatty tissues. Since adipose tissue (fat) determines the size of the breast, you can deduce that one way of enlarging your breasts may be to put on more weight. Should underweight be your problem, have a doctor examine you to determine the cause and take his advice with regard to treatment. In general, proteins and foods rich in carbohydrates help. Exercises such as push-ups, develop the pectoral muscles that lie below the breasts without really increasing their size.

Creams of sex hormones - oestrogen - have been massaged into the breast but without much success. Plastic surgery or silicone injections are not recommended as they leave the breasts very hard and stone-like. Sex hormones, judiciously prescribed by an expert may be of some help, but it is wiser not to interfere with nature.

As far as you are concerned, I would advise a rich

diet; an iron and vitamin tonic to stimulate appetite; and an active, outdoor life. Meanwhile, if you feel too self-conscious about your figure, wear a well-padded, wired bra. Above all, remember that a lithe, healthy body and a sparkling mind are far more attractive than the most perfect vital statistics.

CHAPTER 3

BIRTH OF A VISIONARY

1920s-1930s

World War I, the first conflagration to grip so many nations in its tentacles, had just ended with the signing of the Armistice in November in 1918, thus setting the stage for a brave new world to be ushered in. The contours of the history and geography of Europe were redefined: once great Empires had either been defeated or been obliterated; the borders of many nations were redrawn and new nation-states were constituted; and colonies of European countries stepped up – or initiated – their demand for self-governance and independence. The importance of Europe began to wane, even as the USA's star came on the ascendant.

Within the US, the 'Roaring Twenties' packed in quite a punch, the impact of which was to be felt down the years, worldwide. It was, for the most part, a period of prosperity. The decade marked the onset of the Jazz Age; and the popularisation of the Charleston (a dance criticised by moralists for being of a "sexual nature").

Very importantly too, women in the US gained the right to vote, one more step forward in their struggle for equal rights.

India, then a British colony, saw the launch of the Non-cooperation Movement which took the cry for Independence to the masses and fired the patriotism of vast and differing sections of people across the country.

For the most part, the years of the Twenties decade were marked by peace and prosperity. However, the last year saw a huge downturn in Western economies, beginning with the crash of the stock market in the USA. Very soon, the crisis had a ripple effect on most parts of the globe.

The Great Depression of 1929 as it came to be called, was, arguably, the worst and longest economic downturn that the world has ever witnessed, notwithstanding the financial crisis of 2007-08. It loomed large over the Thirties decade and lasted all the way until 1939 – which year marked the start of another dark and bloody period – the war years of World War II.

Ironically, the 1930s saw an upswing in literature, the arts and films. In fact, it was known as the 'golden age' of Hollywood and saw the production of some classics despite the tough times – or maybe because adversity is the best inspiration for all art. It was also the time when scientific discoveries and progress boomed.

In India, in the 1930s, the cry for 'Purna Swaraj' – complete independence from British rule – emerged.

Across the world, it was a time marked by the people aspiring for self-determination at all levels, whether political or social.

"Every great dream begins with a dreamer. Always remember, you have within you the strength, the patience, and the passion to reach for the stars to change the world."

Harriet Tubman
American abolitionist and socio-political activist

A lot of people across the world believe that children are born under certain stars, and the celestial configuration at the time of birth determines everything from a person's nature, characteristics – even to life choices. Whether Mahinder Chand Wats born on February 11, 1924 to Bhagwant Kaur and her husband Rattan Chand Wats followed the path supposedly plotted by the stars or not, he was certainly a child who reflected and encapsulated all the best of the decade he was born in; while encountering and struggling in the face of some of its drawbacks even decades later.

He was a person who believed deeply in freedom; of the right of the individual to chart his or her own course. Mahinder grew up to be a tolerant and extremely liberal man. He had a deep respect for women and believed implicitly in the equality of the sexes. Yet, he encountered many misogynistic and moralistic attitudes in his working life, all of which he dealt with in his characteristic calm yet firm manner; refusing to be influenced or cowed down by them.

Mahinder Wats was also a very sociable person and loved to interact with people, enjoyed music and dancing and parties, and people associated with him have often remarked about how "westernised" he was. He loved watching films and English films were amongst his favourites.

He grew up to be a person dedicated to the welfare of society and people around him; a fighter for the greater good, for the rights of the individual, he remained till the end undeterred and undeflected in his purpose by hurdles or criticism, or social disapproval. He was, above all, a visionary: a man with a dream, a mission and a passion for his mission.

These were the characteristics which, perhaps, he was born with, but which would blossom over the years and manifest themselves to their fullest degree many decades later. No doubt his intrinsic qualities were also impacted and honed by the early life that he experienced.

Before he reached adulthood, however, there was a vast stretch of terrain covering several years to traverse.

The Wats family seems to have had medicine running through their veins, from earlier generations. Dr. Mahinder Watsa, in the latter years of his life, shared a precious memory of his grandfather Sundermal. "I remember him sitting at those old-fashioned desks in Lahore dispensing medicines to those who sought them," he reminisced. His grandfather was working with the railways, but alternative medicine – unani and ayurvedic it is thought – was his interest, and serving people his passion. So, apart from dispensing medicines at a nominal price or no cost, Grandfather Wats also visited courts and jails where he distributed foodstuff to the wives of those jailed or on trial. They were helpless women and also had children to support, and hence his sympathy was stirred.

In later years, one can glimpse the same sense of generosity, concern and charity in his grandson, Mahinder.

Father Rattan Chand Wats, scion of a well-off family which was by then based in Jalandhar, went to the UK to study medicine and qualified as a doctor. The story goes that by then World War I had broken out, and it was very difficult to get a passage back home as all ships had been requisitioned by the Government for the war effort. He was advised that the only way to return was to join the Army, which would send him on a posting to India. And that is exactly what he ended up doing.

As the ship he was travelling on was passing through the Suez Canal, however, there was a hitch – he was asked to disembark. The reason? The ship had received a message that a doctor was urgently needed to attend to an ailing Colonel T. E. Lawrence, who was then on the African sub-continent engaged in war work for the British. Yes, the same renowned soldier, on whose military exploits, and the book he wrote, *Seven Pillars of Wisdom,* the immensely popular film *Lawrence of Arabia* was based. He was a historic personality in his own right; with many swashbuckling adventures to his credit.

However, when Dr. Wats arrived where the Colonel was stationed to fulfil his assignment, there was much consternation at the camp, to say the least. For, the unit had expected a white doctor not a brown skinned one! It transpired that as time was short, the Quarter Master of the ship, who had been entrusted with the job, plucked out a likely sounding name from the ship's manifest – Lt. R. C. Wats, who he thought was an Englishman as Watts is a common British surname.

Sadly, not much is known or recorded about senior Dr. Wats's encounter with the Lawrence of Arabia, who must have been, arguably, his most famous patient ever. What is known – and has become something of a family legend – is that all ended well, as the patient recovered and was able to get back on duty. Moreover, Dr. Wats' skill and efficiency were much appreciated!

After that little diversion, Lt. (Dr.) Rattan Chand Wats reached Bombay (Mumbai) safely and made it his home and centre from where he made many journeys all over the country and in neighbouring ones as well, over the next several decades.

Rattan Chand's wife, Bhagwant Kaur, came from a middle class family based in Abbottabad, a city now in Pakistan.

Dr. Mahinder Watsa's sister Sheila Khanna recalls the story of how her parents came to be married: "My father was then posted to the Military Hospital in Abbottabad," she narrates. "One day there was a fire in the house where he was staying and he was forced to run out. As he stood in his pyjamas watching the fire engulf his home, sending all his belongings up in smoke, his neighbours rushing to help, came upon the lone man ."

They took the young man – whose acquaintance they had not yet made as he had arrived only recently on his posting – to their home and befriended him. Seeing that he was on his own, his new friends decided to find Dr. Rattan Chand a partner. Living nearby was a family with 10 daughters. The eldest, Bhagwant Kaur was at that time studying medicine in Lady Hardinge Medical College in Delhi. She was peremptorily recalled to Abbottabad to meet the eligible young man. That trip was to put a full stop to her studies, while opening a whole new chapter of her life.

Dr. Rattan Chand had been married earlier when he was only 13 years old. But, he was estranged from his first wife as there was a total lack of compatibility between them, at all levels. Though for several years he had resisted his family's pleas to remarry, fate took a hand that year in Abbottabad. He met the tall and pretty Bhagwant Kaur – and thereby hangs the rest of this story.

Bhagwant Kaur was obviously a more compatible partner to Rattan Chand – not only was she educated and studying medicine when they met, but in time, also proved to be equally matched in other ways too. For, the man who was in the British Army, one who had studied in England moreover, had many different aspects to his personality. As an Army officer, there were too, many social obligations to fulfil. Bhagwant Kaur stood shoulder to shoulder with her husband in the full spectrum of his life.

By all accounts Bhagwant Kaur was a tough, determined and independent woman. She wore pants, drove a car, played tennis, learnt to ride a horse and a cycle and learnt ballroom dancing. She also learnt to bake and cook western dishes.

"My mother had tenacity and guts," Sheila recalls today. "Despite coming from a very orthodox family, she picked up a range of accomplishments and skills an Army officer's wife – especially during the British days – was expected to have."

It was not long before the couple was blessed with a burgeoning family. Apart from Mahinder (fondly called Minny), there was Jitender (better known as Jitty, or simply J) and Rajinder (called Rajin); and a daughter, Sheila, born nine years after the eldest son.

Mahinder Wats was a product of many schools and colleges as his father, an army doctor was liable to be posted to different cities and towns. Hence, the family got a chance to travel all over the country, and to some neighbouring nations too. No doubt his openness, acceptance of a variety of differences amongst human beings and a truly eclectic approach in later life was a result of the exposure to so many different peoples and cultures.

However, at that time, his childhood was much like anyone else's down the ages. Some mischief, some fun, some scrapes and some scoldings, studies and boyish pranks.

For a period of time, the now elevated Colonel Wats was posted at Haffkine Institute in Parel, Mumbai. He was on secondment to the Institute to pursue research activities as, apart from being a doctor, he was a pathologist as well. So, for a while, Mahinder attended St. Mary's School in Mazagaon. The school, established in 1864 by the Society of Jesus (Jesuits) was built next to St. Anne's Church.

In later recollections, he remembers his mother driving him and his brothers to school every morning. "She was a very good mother, but very strict," he says. Narrating an incident that showed exactly how firm and fearless was her nature, he recounts how while driving her sons to school one day, a young boy sprang out of nowhere onto the road and dashed into the car. Fortunately, neither the boy nor the car suffered any damage. But an indignant and Irate Bhagwant Kaur got out and soundly berated the adults accompanying the boy for not taking adequate care of him. Then she got back into the car and calmly drove on.

The young Mahinder seems to have had a close and affectionate relationship with his father. In one of his latter day confidences, he says: "My father was very easy to talk to. He never gave us lectures, but we always had many discussions, especially during our outings."

One memory of school he chuckled over in later years was the method of "settling" disputes. "In school we had a lot of boxing matches," he says euphemistically in his soft even voice with his hallmark understated humour. "If we didn't get on with someone or we had disagreements with them, we would go behind the church after school and settle the matter. There would be fisticuffs."

Though, he adds reassuringly, that method of settling disputes was never repeated by him after school. In fact, as his colleagues say, he was the most calm, peaceful person – always the one to settle disputes, always keeping and making peace, never losing his cool.

On another level, although Mahinder grew up to be a foodie, asparagus was perhaps not top of the charts for him – where once it had been a favourite. For, again, like any other kid there was a time he "over-indulged" to put it mildly.

"Dad and Mum were very social people and were invited out to dinner many a night," narrates Sheila. "On the nights they dined out we children would always be given a choice of what we would like to eat. Minny being the eldest, was given first preference to choose. At that time, he simply loved asparagus and on one occasion, that is what he chose to have. I do not know how many tins of it were opened as Minny made a complete meal of only asparagus. By the time our parents got home, Minny was in the bathroom puking his guts out. So far as I can remember, he never touched asparagus again!"

Later, during their father's continued stint at the Haffkine Institute, Mahinder and Jitender were sent to a boarding school in Simla (Shimla), Bishop Cotton. Considered to be one of the oldest boarding schools for boys not just in India but all of Asia, it prides itself in being the first 'Public School' in the country. It is not clear how long he studied there, but that school too, with its British masters and anglicised environment, must have opened a vista of thought and culture: having an influence on the boy that he was; the man that he became.

At one point of time, Colonel Wats was also posted at a research institute in Kasauli, where the young Mahinder was to have, quite literally, a scarring experience. The family was assigned a beautiful bungalow which stood on a hillside. The house had a large garden which sloped down gently, but at the end of it there was a sudden sharp drop, below which could be seen a bubbling stream.

Along the staff quarters, there were stables – but these were bereft of any horses. Whether a magnanimous father thought to please his son, or the son was enamoured of animals and pleaded for it, one does not know. But when Mahinder was about 12 years old, his father presented him with a beautiful horse. The young Mahinder loved riding and he loved the horse and, from time to time, visited it and offered it treats.

"One day Minny took an apple to feed the horse," recalls Sheila. "He had the apple in the palm of his hand and was about to put his hand out towards the horse when something distracted him and he turned around with the apple still in his hand. Suddenly, he felt himself being lifted off the ground with a sharp excruciating pain in the middle of his back. The horse must have decided: since no apple – let's try a bite of the back! He picked up Minny, and started walking towards the edge of the slope. The horse had got his teeth deep into his flesh. The thousands of people who Minny has helped over the years would have had to live without counselling by the Sexpert, if our gardener had not been around and rescued him. He carried the scar of the bite for the rest of his life."

As he grew older, young Mahinder was enthralled by something which has appealed to many young boys both, before and after him – cars and motorbikes. One day, with typical teenage confidence he decided he would try his hand at driving. After all, how difficult could it be? He had observed people, including his mother, driving cars so often. He crept to the garage, which was at a little distance from the house, got into the car and tried to reverse it out of the garage – and, predictably, went straight into the wall. As it happened, a family acquaintance was passing by at the time, and he shielded the kid from the full wrath of his family descending upon him; offered to teach him driving and promised he would thereafter get a licence for him as well.

That is how Mahinder got his licence when he was in the 9th standard. And, just as he loved riding horses, he loved driving the car. Once, when he was jaunting around town, he was caught by a cop who thought he looked too young to have a licence and flagged down the car. "He even called the Inspector," Dr. Watsa recalled in later years. "But they couldn't do anything – I had a licence and they had no cause to detain me as there was no accident or anything."

Along the way, Colonel Wats was also posted in Rangoon (Yangon) in Burma (Myanmar) and that is where young Mahinder encountered, arguably, one of the most quirky practices he had seen till then.

The family was invited for dinner by the reigning king of the time. The young boy was seated around a huge table, with all the rest of the guests. Soon, Mahinder felt something soft brushing against his feet. After this sensation was repeated a few times, the lad could contain his curiosity no longer. He gently lifted up a portion of the table cloth and looked under it. There, a curious sight greeted his eyes. He saw a line of girls with long hair fanning the feet of all the diners with their tresses. Later, he found out that the strange custom was a way to keep the mosquitoes from attacking the feet of guests. This unique method was apparently routinely practised by the wealthy when entertaining!

When World War II broke out, Colonel Rattan Chand Wats was recalled to active service once again, and was posted in Basra. Eventually, he had to return to India because of an injury. He was then posted as the Commandant of the Military Hospital in Hyderabad where he was to spend several years. For, on retirement from the Army, he took up employment with the Nizam of Hyderabad's Government as Director General of all Jails and Medical Services of the state.

After spending almost a decade working with the Nizam's Government, Mahinder Wats' father returned to Bombay (Mumbai) and headed the Medical Department of the newly set up Bombay Hospital.

By then – actually when Colonel Wats was still in Hyderabad – young Mahinder Wats had joined Grant Medical College in Mumbai. It was the first stop in the journey to his future.

And what a future it proved to be.

FRIEND & GUIDE - 1

In the course of his work with the Family Planning Association of India (FPAI) over several decades, Dr. Mahinder C. Watsa prepared many educative documents addressed to adolescents. These contained not only factual information about the growing years, ranging from physical to emotional changes, each document also ended with some typical questions that might arise and answers to them, providing a veritable map to navigate through the teenage years. What is most noteworthy is the friendly, one-on-one tone of his writings as well as his insight into the typical anxieties and fears of adolescents.

Below are excerpts (slightly rearranged) from:

Bloom and Blossom
Adolescent Guide to Growing Up

A Publication of the Family Planning Association of India (FPAI)

Dear Teenager,
Time has flown and you now stand on the threshold of adulthood. Physical and emotional changes are happening rapidly, and you find yourself in those "in-between years" the first step towards adulthood. You are no longer a child, and yet, not quite an adult. How do you feel? Happy? Confused? Worried? You will want to have the right information about the changes taking place in your body and mind. This booklet has been prepared specially to give you this information. We hope

it will be of help to you. In case you need more information, please feel free to contact the youth friendly centres and staff.

We wish you all the best.

THE GROWING YEARS

GIRLS

Each one of us develops from a child into an adult in his or her own unique way. The "growing-up years", or adolescence, are the most exciting years of your life. This is when you discover new things - about life, people, and most important of all, about yourself. Adolescence (also known as beginning of puberty) is a period of rapid change. It usually occurs between the ages of 10 to 16 years. During this period, both boys and girls experience physical and emotional changes. The changes which take place in girls, including menstruation (commonly called the monthly period), are described here to understand that they are a normal part of growing up. There are also some tips to help you stay fresh and fit during your periods.

Everybody is different!

Each person has his or her own time-clock according to which he or she enters puberty and begins to grow into an adult. In boys, these changes take place at any time between 10-16 years of age. For girls, it can be about a year or so earlier. The changes are caused by the sex hormones which begin to be produced in the testes in boys, and the ovaries in girls. We cannot tell when exactly pubertal changes will begin, but we do know that all boys and girls go through this phase as they mature.

Girls develop at different rates

Just as the time of the onset of puberty varies from one person to another, so also does the rate at which an individual

develops. Each one follows the pattern that is right for his or her own body.

Some of us shoot up rapidly; others take more time. Some of us are tall; some are rounder and shorter. So, don't worry if you are the tallest or shortest; biggest or the smallest; thinnest or heaviest in your class or among your friends.

Remember that every one of us is different, and that an important part of growing up is to learn to like and care for your body, even if it is not exactly what you want.

Emotional changes

As your body develops, so do your feelings. All these changes - physical and emotional - are tied to the hormonal changes that occur during puberty.

Self-love

During this period of growth, you will feel very concerned about how you look, and may spend more time in front of the mirror and in caring for your outward appearance.

Mood swings

You may also tend to become very moody. At times you may feel excited and on top of the world, and at other times, you may feel depressed and think that no one cares for you. You may also have problems with your friends and parents. You may want more freedom resulting in arguments with your parents.

Love amongst the peer group

At this stage in your life, you will want to spend more time with the friends of your age group, and confide in each other.

Attraction towards the opposite sex

As boys and girls grow up, they want to form new friendships with the opposite sex. You may find some boy attractive in your circle of friends, and tend to spend more time with him.

Share your feelings

The mood swings and other emotional and physical changes are a normal part of growing up. Remember, what you are feeling and experiencing happens to everyone else your age. Share your feelings with your mother or older sister, or a female relative or teacher you trust, and who can give you the information and support you need.

GROWING-UP YEARS

BOYS

Physical Changes

There is a sudden increase in height and weight; the shoulders broaden and the muscles begin to grow. The penis and the testicles (or testes) grow larger. One testicle usually hangs lower than the other. This is normal. The testicles begin to produce sperm cells. Hair grows under arms, on arms, and around legs, chest and face, and around penis and testicles (pubic area). The larynx (voice box) grows to adult size and the voice deepens.

(And the section goes on to elaborate from 'Emotional Changes' onwards to the write-up on 'Share Your Feelings' similar to the one above for girls, with suitable changes.)

CHAPTER 4

STEPPING INTO THE FUTURE

1940s

A decade like no other. A period, in the course of which were played out an entire range of emotions and scenarios. From blackest despair to brightest hope. From the most heinous crimes against humanity to the most uplifting stories of bravery and courage. From genocide and massacres to patriotic fervour, liberation and freedom.

Underlying the deafening sound of the crescendo filled years of warfare was the steady beat of life. People going about the business of existence. The evolution of businesses and burgeoning of cultural expression.

Just before the dawn of the decade, in September 1939, Nazi Germany led by Adolf Hitler invaded Poland – and all hell broke loose thereafter. For a period of little over five years, World War II was played out on an even larger canvas than World War I, with even grimmer consequences.

In India, another kind of drama was unfolding. Even as the British continued to deploy Indians as part of the Allied effort in the war, the Independence epic scripted by the nationalists was drawing to a climax.

Once again, the turmoil of the War Years and the end of the period had reshaped political equations between nations and given a focus on new priorities amongst the populace of countries across the globe with several former British and European colonies gaining Independence.

By 1947, India too, had attained Independence from the British Empire after a long, sometimes bloody, struggle.

The stage was set for the young "soneki chidiya" to take flight.

"The future depends on what you do today."

Mahatma Gandhi
Leader of the Indian Freedom Struggle & Proponent of Non-Violence

He strode across the field, a veritable colossus. Tall, well-built, fair, good-looking. Quintessential footballer hero material.

Mahinder Wats may have been studying medicine at Grant Medical College in Mumbai, but he was not only part of its football team, he also captained it for a period. One does not know how many clinical finishes he played, certainly no hospital balls one thinks; but, his was most definitely a class act. For, there was no doubt that he was as much of an impressive and imposing figure and player off-field as on-field.

He was awarded the "Best Cadet" cup for the University Training Corps; and was also a member of the University's tennis and boxing teams.

"He was easily six feet plus, and well built," recalls Dr. Rustom (Rusi) P. Soonawala, the eminent obstetrician-gynaecologist today. "I don't know why he was called 'Minny' – there was nothing diminutive about him."

It was not only Dr. Watsa's physical appearance that was so arresting; his was an exceedingly charismatic personality as well. Numerous friends and colleagues have stressed time and again how he had such a towering, larger-than-life commanding presence which would always dominate any gathering.

By the time the young Mahinder Wats was ready to commence his medical training, there was an entire section of Indian society educated in institutions set up by the British and other groups from the Western world – either the British Government itself; or by Jesuits and other orders from different countries.

At the time, there was a kind of cultural ethos which bound a certain section of society – English speaking, exposed to western culture, including art, music, dance. They had a vast exposure to western thought through myriad books and this opened entirely new horizons for them. In economic terms, this section of Indian society of the time largely came from richer, better off families, which had accumulated their wealth through business, trade, or as skilled professionals – either self-employed or in high paying jobs.

So, in a manner of speaking, it was only natural that the Soonawala brothers (there were four of them, all of whom took up medicine, following in the footsteps of their father Dr. Phiroze Soonawala) and Mahinder C. Wats (whose father was also a doctor) should become friends.

Though he himself was three years junior to them, Dr. Rusi Soonawala recounts how his elder brother, the late Dr. Jamshed P. Soonawala and Dr. Watsa were of the same age and good friends since their days in medical college.

In the years to come, Dr. Rusi Soonawala, who took up the same specialisations as Dr. Watsa, would continue his close association and friendship with Dr. Watsa till the very end of the latter's life. So much so, that "Rusi Uncle" continues to be a prominent figure in the life of the Watsa family even today.

The Grant Medical College, one of the foremost educational institutions of its time, was set up through the strenuous efforts of a former Governor of Bombay, Sir Robert Grant, who unfortunately passed away before he could see the first batch of students walking in through its portals – or for that matter even learn that he had received approval for his proposal.

This was the second attempt at establishing an institution in Bombay (Mumbai) to train Indians in the field of medical sciences. Around 1840 only two medical institutions existed – one in Calcutta (Kolkata) and one in Madras (Chennai).

The Grant Medical College building was completed in 1845 with the first batch of students being admitted in November of that year. This was almost exactly a century prior to Dr. Watsa's taking admission there.

On the same premises, adjacent to the college, another building was constructed. Originally built as the 'School of Practice' – with funding from Sir Jamsetjee Jejeebhoy – it has today developed into the humongous, multi-facility J.J. Hospital, administered by the State of Maharashtra.

Though the early part of the 20th century witnessed much turmoil and churn, and even while WWII was playing itself out elsewhere, within India there were a number of streams flowing simultaneously – while one section of the populace backed the British foray in the war and the large deployment of Indian soldiers; a powerful section spearheaded by the Indian National Congress demanded that India be first given its Independence before it joined the War effort. Towards that goal, the Indian National Congress (INC) launched the Quit India movement on August 8, 1942 from what is today called August Kranti Maidan in Mumbai.

Almost immediately, virtually the entire leadership of the Congress was imprisoned, and the Quit India movement was effectively crushed with the British Government refusing to give in to the demands of the INC. The position of the British Government in India was that independence could only be thought about after the war ended. However, to avoid further conflagration, they did make some future commitments to the INC. This situation remained the status quo for several years.

The war ended in 1945, and the process of transfer of power began thereafter, based on the commitment made by the British, who had emerged from WWII as a considerably weakened force. The sun which had never set on the British Empire seemed all set to take a dip.

Yet, on the other hand, life had carried on as usual for a lot of the young men and women of the country. Amongst them was this budding band of friends, including the Soonawala brothers and Mahinder Watsa, who were destined to become great men of the medical profession and luminaries in their chosen fields.

Though at that time, in their youth, there was also the pursuit of adventure and fun times.

"In those days, our main aim was to own a motorcycle," reminisces Dr. Soonawala. "Watsa used to sit behind my brother and we would go for long rides – to Khopoli to eat biryani; on weekends we would go off as a group to Khandala, Lonavala or Poona. We were all like-minded and we enjoyed the same things."

As he recalls, those were prohibition days and exclaims: "It was fun having a drink during prohibition!"

Perhaps that was when Mahinder's love for motorcycles and all they represented began. In later years he recounted how he used to speed around on his bike, including when dating his future bride. "Two-three times, I have also skidded and fallen off," he said. "Once I even slid under a tram! But I was lucky as the tram was stationary and I got away without any serious injuries."

At this point in his life, there was another major development in young Mahinder's life. When he had taken admission to study medicine in Grant Medical College, his father was not in Mumbai but posted in Hyderabad; hence, he was put up at the residence of old and dear family friends – the Motwanes.

Now, how the two families met is a story in itself – one scripted by fate and shaped by destiny.

One day, senior Dr. Wats (Rattan Chand) was returning by car from out of town and got a flat tyre on the way. Just then, another car passed by, bearing members of the Motwane (of Chicago Radio fame) family, who were also returning to Bombay (Mumbai) from out of town. "Seeing a smart looking gentleman struggling to fix a flat tyre they stopped to offer help," recalls Sheila, Dr. Watsa's sister. Thus, began a friendship between the two families which would prove to be not only long lasting; but also one which would, in time, be transformed into a close family relationship.

Originally from Larkana in the Sindh Province of Pakistan, Gianchand

Chandumal Motwane, the founder of the family business was a shrewd businessman. His is a fascinating story imbued with the spirit of dauntless enterprise. He began working as a book binder at the tender age of 12 when he was left fatherless; by the age of 31, in 1909, he had set up his own business under the name of Eastern Electric & Trading Co. After a decade of nimble entrepreneurship covering a variety of businesses – and taking the war years of WWI in stride – Gianchand set up Chicago Telephone Supply Co. in 1919 in Mumbai. He went on to become the first broadcaster in India, changed the name of his Mumbai-based company to Chicago Telephone & Radio Co., which was eventually transformed to a limited liability company in 1939.

Though Gianchand himself passed away at the age of 65 in 1943, he had made his two sons Visharam and Nanik partners in 1937 (and in due course two grandsons also joined the company) so the business continued to prosper and expand. Eventually, in 1958 the two companies were amalgamated under the banner of Motwane Private Limited.

By the time partition took place, the Motwanes had already established a strong base in Mumbai, India, with a business spread to many cities within the country. Hence, though they lost their businesses and property situated in what became Pakistan, they did not face much of a problem like many other families from Sind who came to India as refugees. On an aside, interestingly, the Motwane home in Larkana was taken over by the Bhuttos (specifically, by Benazir's grandfather it is said).

Nanik Motwane, Gianchand's younger son, was an ardent believer of Indian Independence and a Congressman. He was a participant in the freedom struggle at many levels and was even jailed as a result. In fact, as the family legend goes, once when he was arrested, he went to jail with black hair and came back with it turned completely white!

However, be that as it that may, in 1929, when the struggle was waging strong, though Independence was still many years away, Nanik Motwane, then the Company's Managing Director had observed: "I saw

Gandhiji going from platform to platform to address meetings at one and the same place, to enable his weak voice to be heard by large numbers. It was then that I felt that I must find some means to amplify his voice."

He managed to achieve just that when his company went on to produce public address systems under the brand name of Chicago Radio. Both the public address systems as well as the broadcasting foray (introduced by his father) went on to strengthen the voices of the leaders of the freedom struggle and carry their words to a vast population which would have been otherwise difficult to reach.

In the house of this freedom fighter were born six children – two girls and four boys. The eldest of them, Promila, was a young, lissom, budding beauty when Mahinder Wats came to study in Mumbai and took up residence with the large joint family of the Motwanes.

Though the families had known each other intimately for a long time, and the young Mahinder and Promila were undoubtedly acquainted earlier, this meeting afresh must have sparked a new interest in each other. For, no longer young children or awkward adolescents, they had both entered their youth now. By all accounts, it was the handsome, strapping Mahinder who was quite, quite smitten first; and he spent many a month wooing her. But, Promila was slow to respond. Whatever the reason for the damsel to demur, demur she did.

Now, the young Mahinder, with the world at his feet, was nothing if not dogged and persistent. So, he kept wooing the woman he loved, trying every way of breaking down her reserve. Even after he graduated from college and left the Motwane residence, he would often go and visit Promila at her family home in Khar.

Promila was a very gentle, sociable person loved by all. Dr. Watsa, just before he passed away, casting his mind back, recalled the days he was "courting" her. "I would drive up to visit her taking my dog with me – he was a very large creature," he reminisced. "I would park my car a few houses away from where they lived, and the moment I opened the door, the dog would go bounding off and head straight to Promila. I would find him in her room, wagging his tail, when I reached!"

Eventually, the lady relented. And, like a fairytale ending, Promila finally said "Yes".

Except, quite unknown to all, young Mahinder Wats' life at that point was poised not so much at the conclusion of a romantic story, but the beginning of an epic tale.

Meanwhile, there was one more significant development which took place around this time. Just as his father Col. R. C. Wats had been once taken for an Englishman based on his name, Mahinder was often mistaken for an Anglo-Indian when in Medical College. In his case, apart from the name, there was also his fair colouring, his impressive frame, and his decided good looks.

At some point, when he was at Grant Medical, he requested his father's permission to change his name from 'Wats' to 'Watsa', hoping that emphasis on the 'a' at the end would make it more Indian sounding. Whether it indeed accomplished its purpose or not one doesn't know, but Watsa it has remained – for Dr. Mahinder C. Watsa as well as his immediate family which has come after him.

Just before the conclusion of the decade, in 1949, an organisation was registered in India, which would have a far-reaching impact in the field of reproductive and sexual health – the Family Planning Association of India (FPAI). It would also be the ideal vehicle for Dr. Watsa to proliferate his message and mission, which was to develop over the course of the next few decades.

For the moment, however, the young Mahinder was busy concluding his stint as a medical student, preparing for the next stage of his journey into the future.

FRIEND & GUIDE -2

It was not only detailed physical and emotional information that the various booklets, produced for FPAI, imparted to the young readers, but they also touched upon other issues and social problems related to the youth. No doubt these publications must have often helped to clarify matters confusing youngsters; and not just for them, but also for their parents, who those days would have been equally without the information resources to steer through the stormy seas of their children's teenage years.

More importantly, in these pronouncements too, one can glimpse the forward thinking nature of Dr. Mahinder C. Watsa who had set the agenda for the content in his days.

Continuing the excerpts from:

Bloom and Blossom

Adolescent Guide to Growing Up

A Publication of the Family Planning Association of India (FPAI)

GENDER, SEX AND SEXUALITY

Gender

Gender is social expectations of society. Both girls and boys should be treated equally. Boys and girls are equally capable and can do similar work. Gender is a socially defined idea about masculinity or male roles and femininity or female roles. Gender roles are learned. They are not innate or 'natural'. In fact, everything males can do, females can also do. And almost everything that females do, males can also do.

Sex

Sex is the difference in biological characteristics of males and females. Sex is universal across the world. Treat persons of every sex with respect and dignity.

Sexuality

Sexuality is a natural and healthy part of living. Individuals and society benefit when children are able to discuss sexuality with their parents and/or other trusted adults. Sexuality is how people experience and express themselves as sexual beings. Sexuality includes physical, ethical, spiritual, social, psychological and emotional dimensions.

ALCOHOL AND SUBSTANCE ABUSE

Addiction is a complex disorder characterised by compulsive drug use. People who are addicted feel an overwhelming, uncontrollable need for drugs or alcohol, even in the face of negative consequences. This self-destructive behaviour can be hard to understand. The answer lies in the brain. Repeated drug use alters the brain causing long-lasting changes to the way it looks and functions. These brain changes interfere with your ability to think clearly, exercise good judgement, control your behaviour, and feel normal without drugs. These changes are also responsible, in large part, for the drug cravings and compulsion to use that make addiction so powerful.

TYPES OF DRUG ABUSE

Alcohol: Some symptoms of dependence on alcohol are shakiness, nausea, rapid heartbeat, sweating and anxiety. Alcohol damages your liver, brain and heart. Tests show that an alcoholic's brain reacts differently to alcohol than a non-alcoholic's.

Nicotine: Nicotine encourages users to smoke or chew tobacco more. When people smoke, it changes the way their mind

works so that they need the nicotine again and again.

Drugs: Many drugs abused are illegal but some are prescription drugs. Some are made from plants. It is easy to become addicted to illegal drugs. Marijuana, heroin, cocaine, ecstasy and crack are all illegal drugs that people often become addicted to. Even some prescription drugs are addictive. Just don't start taking drugs because it is really hard to break the habit. Once the drug is in your system, your body gets so used to it that you might need that drug to function properly. Another way drugs are made is in a lab; these drugs are called designer drugs. There are many types of designer drugs available. They can be classified as: stimulants, opiates, and hallucinogenic. Most designer drugs are extremely addictive and young people do not realise this. Most of these drugs are inhaled, injected, or taken orally as a tablet.

Inhalants: A drug that enters the body through breathing is an inhalant. Inhalants are more commonly used by teenagers. Inhalants can be found in industrial or household products, including paint thinners or removers, degreasers, dry-cleaning fluids, gasoline, and lighter fluid, art or office supply solvents, including correction fluids, felt-tip marker fluid, electronic contact cleaners, glue, household aerosol propellants in items such as spray paints, hair or deodorant sprays, fabric protector sprays, aerosol computer cleaning products, and vegetable oil sprays, ether, chloroform, halothane and nitrous oxide ("laughing gas"), etc.

HOW ADDICTION DEVELOPS

The path to drug addiction starts with experimentation. You or your loved one may have tried drugs out of curiosity, because friends were doing it, or in an effort to erase another problem.

At first, the substance seems to solve the problem or make life better, so you use the drug more and more. But as the addiction progresses, getting and using the drug becomes more and more important and your ability to stop using it is compromised.

What begins as a voluntary choice turns into a physical and psychological need. The good news is that drug addiction is treatable. With treatment and support, one can counteract the disruptive effects of addiction and regain control of one's life.

HOW TO SAY NO ALCOHOL AND DRUGS

Make a joke: Sometimes humour is the best way to respond to a situation, as it can lighten a serious mood. It can also divert attention away from you onto something else.

Give a reason why it's bad: Maybe you can't smoke because you want to be able to run the mile for the track team. Maybe you don't want to drink because you know someone who is an alcoholic and you can see how drinking has messed up their life. Backing up your refusal with evidence gives it more power.

Make an excuse why you can't: Maybe you have something else to do that will interfere. Or you have to be somewhere at a specific time. Or your mom will kill you. Whatever. But say it and stick to it. Just say no, plainly and firmly. In some situations, just saying no without a lot of arguing and explaining is the best response. Just make sure your "no" is a strong and determined one.

Suggest an alternative activity: Lots of kids wind up doing stuff they shouldn't because they lack proper options. They're bored. Try thinking of something better to do, offering everyone an "out". You just might be surprised who might take you up on it.

Ignore the suggestion: Pretend you didn't hear it, and change the topic to something else. Act like you don't think the idea was even worth discussing.

Repeat yourself if necessary: Sometimes it takes more than once, on more than one occasion. Just because someone asks more than once, that doesn't mean that you have to cave.

Leave the situation: If you don't like where things are headed, you can take off. It might seem risky, but with you leading the way, other kids who really don't want to do it either just may follow you.

Thanks, but no thanks: You can be polite, but you still aren't interested. It just isn't something you are into.

The power of numbers: Make a pact with your friends to stick to your guns. Often, knowing that your friends will back you up can help you feel more comfortable being assertive. Sometimes "we" feels stronger than "I".

Have the courage to say "NO": Also remember that taking eatables, drinks or any gifts from strangers can lead you to serious trouble.

CHAPTER 5

THE BRAVE NEW WORLD

1950s-1960s

A time to look ahead. A time to put the horrors of war behind and to rebuild lives and nations; economies and polities; societies and cultures.

It was boomtime in the West, especially in the USA which had emerged as the leading industrial and political power on the globe. Life was good; life was enjoyable. But, most of all, Life needed to be affirmed. The result was a hitherto unseen baby boom, especially in the US.

It was the period when classic pop made way for rock-n-roll and legion are the names of the top music sensations of the '50s decade including Bing Crosby, Nat King Cole, Elvis Presley and Chuck Berry. Television which had already made an entry grew bigger and more widespread.

In America it was also a time when changing gender roles caused some upheaval on the social front, and in the realm of sexual mores.

The year 1950 marked one of the most significant milestones in the history of Indian Independence: January 26, the day the people of the country took unto itself the Constitution of India.

Within the country there was a euphoric atmosphere bringing out – by and large – the best in people as they went about building a new India.

It was a time when the youth all over the world and the citizens of the young nation, India, held dreams in their eyes, and hope in their heart. And the magic of that sense of exhilaration touched one and all; and was imbued in whatever they did.

"The best way to predict your future is to create it."

Abraham Lincoln

American Statesman & Former President of the USA

One can imagine a young, eager Dr. Mahinder Watsa, in the year 1950, perched like an explorer on a peak, eyes shaded looking ahead. As if hoping to catch a glimpse of the contours his life would follow in the vista spread out before him.

Just as it was for the rest of the world, and particularly his home country India, the 1950s were a time of fresh beginnings for Dr. Watsa, too, in more ways than one.

On the one hand, he stepped into a new phase of his chosen career path – it marked the end of his student years and a stepping onto the first rung of the ladder as a man of healing.

It was in 1950 that the young doctor began practising in the real world. He soon secured the position of Registrar in Obstetrics and Gynaecology at the Nair Hospital.

Dr. Saroj Jha who was then a student of the TN Medical College (attached to the Hospital) in Bombay, shares a memory: "I must say that the new handsome and dashing Registrar turned many female heads, including mine!" she recalls with a laugh now. "But as convention demanded, we had to keep our distance."

As her father was a senior doctor attached to Nair Hospital, and a friend of the senior Dr. Soonawala, their children were also acquainted since childhood. A connect that proved to be useful for the much younger Saroj to later become part of a large social group.

She recalls with a smile in her voice, "I was lucky. My connections with the Soonawala brothers, Rusi and Fardoon worked. I got introduced to Dr. Watsa and soon became part of his social group which had the Soonawala brothers and Dr. Watsa at its core."

It was a fun group that enjoyed the music of the times and swayed to the tunes of the 1950s. "We led a very active social life," Dr. Jha reminisces. "We listened to Bing Crosby songs and other music of those days, and we danced – the waltz and the foxtrot were the popular dances at that time. Dr. Watsa loved music, loved dancing, loved parties – he was a very sociable person."

She adds: "That was the beginning of my association with Dr. Watsa and the start of what grew to become a close friendship that spanned several decades."

However, it seems that doctors were not then, as they are not now, content to rest on singular laurels. There is a constant thirst for procuring additional qualifications: and many continue to either pursue more degrees in their chosen field; or go on to get qualified in allied or additional areas. Both were true of our budding medical professional, the young Dr. Watsa.

Even as he was associated with Nair Hospital, Dr. Watsa went ahead to acquire a Diploma in Child Health (DCH). He was now in a good position to practice as a family doctor, with the emphasis being on women and children.

On the personal front, we left him in the last chapter with the woman of his dreams having finally yielded to his wooing, "acquiescing his suit", as the British might have said in those days.

"The course of true love never did run smooth", had bemoaned the hero of a popular play by Shakespeare. In our story, the initial rough patches had been posed by Promila's resistance to Mahinder's advances. One would have thought that once there was acceptance and a mutual sharing of their feelings for each other, the road to marriage would be a relatively short and trouble-free one. Especially as their two families had been such close friends for many, many years by then. Hadn't Mahinder been sent to live with the Motwanes while he pursued his medical education? But, no! Things were not as simple and smooth as all that.

Unexpectedly, the objection came not from her family – all of whom were quite happy as their relationship was about to be changed into marriage – but from his mother. The strong, independent Bhagwant Kaur, who had scripted a new story for herself, still retained in a small corner of her consciousness a short chapter on traditions and traditional perspectives, which couldn't quite align with the thought of a Sindhi daughter-in-law.

Moreover, one must remember that those were the days of arranged marriages. A time when young men and women waited meekly for their families to choose a life partner for them.

So, the fact that Mahinder Watsa held out for a "love marriage" made a statement which spoke volumes both about his outlook and his personality. The same could be said for Promila. For, if it was unusual for a man to make such a decision, and stick by it in the face of opposition, it was almost impossible for a woman to exert her own will those days.

"Despite coming from different backgrounds and castes – Minny being a Punjabi Brahmin and Promila a Sindhi – and also besides going against the tradition of arranged marriages, they were eventually married," says Mahinder's sister Sheila.

And so, on December 14, 1951 the two were joined together as husband and wife, after overcoming all resistance to their marriage.

Even after all these decades, Dr. Indira Kapoor is still full of admiration for what she deems to be have been a courageous act, though today it might not seem to be all that much of a big deal. She says, stressing emphatically: "He had a love marriage as early as in 1951. At that time only the brave and the bold could do that – choose their own partners."

A newly minted doctor and a freshly minted husband, Dr. Mahinder Watsa soon settled into the rhythm of his new life. And life was good. It was exciting. There was a world out there to be conquered.

Promila, for her part, also eagerly took to setting up home in the Nair Hospital staff quarters assigned to the young doctor. Though they must have been a far cry from her large and luxurious parental home, there was never the faintest of frowns on her brow; or the slightest whisper of a complaint on her lips.

Almost exactly three years after they were married, the couple became the proud parents of a baby boy, Gautam, on December 11, 1954.

In those days, it was virtually a tradition for young, newly qualified doctors who had received their basic degrees in medicine – and, one must add, who came from the elite strata of society – to go abroad for further studies.

"Everybody at that time had the ambition to go to the UK or the US, after they finished their residencies," explains Dr. Soonawala. "I also went to the UK – Mahinder was already there, as was my elder brother Jamshed, with whom he was still very close."

However, Dr. Watsa's stay in the UK in the first instance was cut short due to the failing health of his father. As both father and son were keen to meet each other, Dr. Mahinder Watsa returned to Mumbai with his family.

Though, after his father's demise at the end of 1956, he did go back to England for a brief while to complete all that he had set out to accomplish there, Dr. Watsa was soon back at Sunder House, the building which had earlier been purchased in its entirety by his father.

That is the place where his family first set up home on his return to Mumbai from the UK – and that was the place where he lived out the final few decades of his life and breathed his last.

While in the UK, Dr. Watsa had also acquired a DObst RCOG (Diploma of the Royal College of Obstetricians and Gynaecologists).

By this time, the young doctor had an impressive string of qualifications after his name and an equally impressive range of hospitals he had practised or attended in.

He had held House Surgeonships in obstetrics and gynaecology, general surgery, and medicine in India and the UK. He had held a Registrarship in Obstetrics & Gynaecology at the B. Y. L. Nair Hospital, Bombay (Mumbai); had held the post of Residential Medical Officer in Nowrosjee Wadia Maternity Hospital, Bombay (Mumbai); and had chalked up post-graduate attendance at the J. J. Group of Hospitals Bombay (Mumbai), and at Bai Jerbai Wadia Hospital for Children, Bombay (Mumbai); and at Hammersmith Hospital, London in Obstetrics & Gynaecology. He had also served as Medical Officer in charge of Bhabha Hospital, Bandra, Mumbai from 1955-56.

In the interregnum between the two periods that the Mahinder Watsa family lived in Sunder House, they lived in Bandra in company accommodation. This is how it came about.

On his return from the UK, he was presented with the intriguing and interesting opportunity of gaining experience at a corporate level at the medicine manufacturing conglomerate Glaxo Laboratories (India) Limited. He took up a job with the company starting out on March 1, 1957 as an Executive in the Medical Research Division.

Initially, his brief was to write the medical literature, keep tabs on information appearing in medical journals, train medical representatives (including by delivering lectures on medical subjects), and to handle queries on products raised by doctors. His work also required him to attend various medical conferences. More importantly, he was part of the committee which was responsible for formulating the marketing strategy for the company's products.

Though he had joined the company in the Medical Department in the first instance, his bosses Mr. D. J. R. Farrant and Mr. Thompson spotted a special spark in him. They thought he would do very well in Marketing & Sales and in administrative positions and therefore sent him to attend special courses. Thus it was that Dr. Mahinder C. Watsa added yet other skills to his quiver – those of marketing and management.

However, the training was to stand him in good stead in the years to come as well; not merely during his assignment with Glaxo, but also later when he worked with large organisations where his organising skills were very helpful.

Today, his colleagues remember Dr. Watsa's 360-degree accomplishments with awe. Not only was he an excellent doctor, with accurate diagnostic skills; he also possessed great charisma and enjoyed a wonderful connect with his patients. Moreover, he was extremely knowledgeable about his subject; and was also an organiser and administrator par excellence, a man born with great leadership qualities.

By 1962, Dr. Watsa had risen in the esteem of the senior management and in the ranks of the company too. He was appointed as the Head of the Clinical Research Department, which, in fact, was created as a result of his efforts.

The setting up of the department opened a new horizon for the doctor in terms of broadening his experience, widening his network and also honing and deepening his management skills. In this capacity he not only initiated clinical research on new products as well as on existing ones for newer indications, he did the follow up on the publications of the clinicians and researchers in medical journals across the country, too.

He was also tasked with attending major medical conferences held in the country and thus became acquainted with a wide cross-section of doctors across India. In fact, he went on to become one of the prime founder members of the Association of Medical Advisers to the Pharmaceutical Industry. Having successfully established the department, Dr. Watsa was next appointed as Manager of the Medical Research Division in 1964, thus becoming responsible for managing the entire medical policy of the Company. He prepared the budgets both for research activities, as well as medical promotions and was tasked with ensuring that there was a proper spending spread – across medical research, scholarships, clinical trials, and so on.

Dr. Watsa was a valued member of the Sales Director's team and assisted in formulating the Company's overall marketing policy. On the other hand, he was actively involved in the clinical research area as well. And, importantly, he planned and organised several conferences for Medical Representatives.

The experience of organising conferences was to stand him in good stead going ahead, both in terms of understanding their intrinsic importance as a platform for spreading knowledge, as well as learning about tackling the nitty-gritty for a successful conference.

Dr. Vikram Sharma who was his colleague in Glaxo had joined the company a few years after Dr. Watsa did. He describes the Medical Department as the "spine" of the company at that time.

"We first got together in the Clinical Trials Department, of which Minny had just taken charge when I joined Glaxo around 1962-63," says Dr. Sharma.

The next stop on Dr. Watsa's upward trajectory in Glaxo was in temporary assignments over a one-year period of (1967-68) as Manager of the Calcutta (Kolkata) and Delhi branches of the Company. These were followed by the important posting as Manager of the Bombay Branch where he did such a splendid job that at the end of the Glaxo India's 1970-71 sales year, the branch won the coveted 'Top of League Trophy' of the Glaxo Pharmaceutical Division, for having clocked the highest sales; that too, with a commanding lead over its nearest competitor, the Madras (Chennai) branch. It was a proud moment indeed when the trophy was presented by Mr. Farrant, then Glaxo's Managing Director to Dr. Watsa.

The late Albert C. de Souza, a former Glaxo colleague (who recently passed away, before this book was released) had earlier remarked: "When we knew he was coming as Branch Manager to the Bombay Branch, we wondered how he would fit in. As someone quipped, he was moving from Caesarean Section to 'Sales General Section'! However, he proved himself adept in a new field. He brought a new approach to handling people."

So competent did Dr. Watsa prove to be at the job as the Manager of the Bombay Branch, that he was promoted as the All India Sales Manager in 1971.

After spending a very valuable and successful 16 years with Glaxo, Dr. Watsa decided to resign from the Company in early 1973 and concentrate on his main interests – medical practice, counselling and spreading medical knowledge and sex education amongst the youth.

Even in the few months before he left, he was asked to start a new department – the New Products Development Division – which was to have an important role in the company's future growth. Characteristically, Dr. Watsa took on the challenge, and completed his task successfully.

At a farewell function held in Dr. Watsa's honour, Mr. Thompson, the then Sales Director said that he had made very useful contributions to every area in which he had worked. As a medical man he had helped Glaxo to maintain the delicate balance between what was required by the medical profession and what was good for the profitability of the company. As a Manager he had motivated his staff to work towards a common goal and had encouraged individual development, he stressed.

After his resignation, Dr. Watsa continued to be in touch with Glaxo in an advisory capacity and made his expert services available for the Representatives Training Programme.

This was preliminary to his stepping into the next phase of his life and career, which, without doubt, was his most successful stint in terms of accomplishments, achievements and satisfaction. He may not have known it, or been conscious about it but he was ready to launch an assault on the peak of his career.

Meanwhile, the friendship and connection with the Soonawala family had blossomed further. Around the late 1950s, Dr. Rusi Soonawala had also returned to Mumbai after a spell in the UK. "When I came back, I was working at Wadia hospital as a junior consultant between 1956 and 1963," recalls Dr. Soonawala. "Dr. Watsa was also working at Wadia hospital for some time during this period but in another unit. At that time, we had a lot of interaction – we saw each other's patients and discussed our cases constantly."

He recalls Dr. Watsa as being very soothing and much like a father figure to his patients. "He always gave the right advice and never tried to fool the patient or relatives – he was very honest," says Dr. Soonawala.

Dr. Watsa's honesty was all-encompassing and his hallmark throughout his career. Dr. Soonawala explains saying: "Nowadays there are many malpractices; doctors who might lead the patients on. Also, those days there was a feeling that if you bribed doctors, you could get better treatment. But we were never tempted to be dishonest. Fortunately, we were OK financially."

He adds: "Apart from being family friends, there was a far greater bond binding us. We were like-minded, had the same approach. We were not after money – we were only concerned about our patients, their care and our work."

On the work front, while Dr. Watsa was at Glaxo he was associated with developing various new products. Around that time, Dr. Rusi Soonawala had designed an intrauterine device. "Population growth was a matter of concern and contraception was being emphasised in a big way. I designed this intrauterine device and named it S IUD – as in Soonawala IUD. Chandrakant Garware had helped me in making it. Dr. Watsa was keen for me to introduce it in the market and had also arranged a meeting with his boss who was an Englishman. I met the gentleman twice in London; but unfortunately, nothing came of it – the American patents were very tough to fight."

However, to back pedal a bit. Even when he joined Glaxo and set out on the corporate path, the medical profession was Dr. Watsa's first passion. He had an understanding with the Glaxo management that he could continue with his private practice.

Thus it came about that two years after he joined the company, Dr. Mahinder Watsa acquired a cottage with a small compound on Hill Road at Bandra, and set up his own independent clinic in 1959 to establish his practice as a Family Doctor. "Dad's clinic was at 79, Hill Road in a little cottage," remembers Gautam. "Here he was assisted by May, who was a qualified nurse. She was quite a battle-axe, a strict disciplinarian and kept both Dad and the patients in check. Nothing escaped her sharp eyes and ears. In the latter years Dad felt the need to bring in a pathologist at the clinic to facilitate pathological tests, so Mr. Naik, a very soft-spoken gentleman was brought in."

Dr. Sharma has his own memories of the clinic as well. "Minny and I had become friends and he invited me to join his clinic," he says. "He had a clear understanding with the company that he could run his clinic; and I joined him in my free time."

No telling of Dr. Mahinder C. Watsa's story would be complete, indeed would be lacking that particular spicy flavour, if one did not recount the very extraordinary connection he had with a community of fisherfolk then living in Bhayander. What is more, different people in Dr. Watsa's life have different anecdotes to relate about his very special relationship with them.

Sometime in the 1960s, Dr. Watsa began visiting Bhayander as a consultant, one day a week.

"Now it so happened that a few ladies were having trouble conceiving," narrates Gautam. "After consulting with him, in the initial days of his practice there, all these ladies, without exception conceived within a few months and carried the babies to full term. Dad was their miracle doctor – and to top it all, each of the ladies gave birth to a healthy baby boy. You can imagine the jubilation when this happened. So much so, that one of the ladies who had conceived after 10 years, actually named her first born son Watsa."

This news spread like wildfire to the surrounding areas of Uttan, as far as Dongri Chowk and further. As a result, he got several patients from these areas too, subsequently. His reputation as a doctor spread quickly in the community and he was not just widely respected, but also revered.

"After this, these fisherfolk would come all the way to Dad's clinic for any medical problem," continues Gautam. "He always had a cure for them; and in case necessary, would refer them to another doctor. Their appreciation knew no bounds and ever so often on a Sunday early morning they would arrive at our house at Shivaji Park with baskets full of fish and prawns."

One particular Sunday morning the doorbell rang at about 5 a.m. "All of us jumped out of bed wondering who was at our door," remembers Gautam. "We could only see about six to seven hefty men on the staircase. Mom initially said, 'Don't open the door!' To cut a long story short, when we opened the door and let them in, we found that it was Nadrish Patil from Dongri Chowk and his relatives carrying a fish which was about seven feet long. It turned out to be a swordfish which they had brought as a gift for Dad as this was the first time any of them had caught such a fish!"

There is one other memory that will remain with Gautam as well as his wife always. He says: "When Deepa and I were getting married, virtually the entire village showed up bringing with them their band to play in the *baraat*!"

When Dr. Watsa was no longer able to continue going to Bhayander due to his other responsibilities, the fisherfolk would come to Bandra to consult him, travelling great distances. They would sit patiently outside in the compound for long periods till it was time for him to come to the clinic. It was a sight that soon became familiar to all his other patients who hailed from a broad spectrum of society and included not only a vast number of professionals and middle class families, but also some celebrities from Bollywood and other artistic circles.

Speaking of the fisherfolk, Dr. Sharma remarks, "Their loyalty was quite touching."

It so happened that to some extent, their benevolent feelings radiated outwards to people associated with Dr. Watsa and his clinic too.

Dr. Sharma recalls one such incident. "One day, one of the patients turned up late, and continued to remain seated even after everyone had left," he narrates. "I was a bit puzzled but didn't say anything. Then, once the last person had left, she quickly cleared and set the table, and served me some fish curry she had prepared and brought all the way to the clinic to express her gratitude and appreciation."

He adds: "The kind of affection that people had for him and as a result, for all of us too, was something rarely seen."

Then there was an incident narrated by Dr. Watsa himself to his assistant, Trishla Jain, in later years. Needless to say, this one was underlined with his trademark tongue-in-cheek humour. One evening, he said, he was attending a wedding of one of the fisherfolk, and moving around meeting people, many of whom he was familiar with. In the middle of a conversation he heard one woman at some distance from where he was. She was pointing to him and excitedly and loudly telling a young boy who was standing by her side: "See that man over there? He is the person responsible for you being here today!" Needless to say, she was one of his patients who had successfully borne a son. But the manner in which she said this in the middle of a large gathering was a bit disconcerting. "I was so embarrassed," recalled Dr. Watsa with a chuckle.

Heartwarming and amusing in turn though his experiences might have been on one hand, there was another, more troubling facet to them as well. He would often remark that it was in the 1950s, in the course of his practice, that he began to realise what a lacuna existed in the information available to young people, particularly girls, and to what extent they suffered as a result.

In one of his profiles describing his experiences, he says about himself (in the third person in the original):

"In the early '50s he was disturbed by the widespread prevalence of gender violence, unhappiness and separations in couple relationships and persons with sexual concerns being relieved of their money by quacks."

Though he acquired much acclaim and got to be known widely thanks to his *Mumbai Mirror* column, few people might be aware that he began his column writing as early as in the 1950s.

The first column that he did was for a magazine published by Frene Talyarkhan called *Trend*. The publication was, as its name suggests, more about fashion and other similar topics and aimed mainly at women. Talyarkhan approached him to do a health column for the magazine, titled '*The Doctor Says*'. The intention of this column was not to discuss sexual issues but to focus on health matters.

Yet, as Dr. Watsa recounted in the film made on him, increasingly, he began to receive very disturbing letters – women who had been subjected to rape worried that their husbands-to-be might discover that they were not virgins; victims of incest who were traumatised; either one of couples who was unfulfilled and unhappy in their relationship, and so on.

Sometime later, he was invited to do a column for *Femina,* then the leading women's magazine from *The Times of India* stable. This column, under the name '*Doctor Talks to You*', ran for around 10-15 years and only went to reinforce his observations from his *Trend* column. He was inundated with letters from people suffering similar problems: "distressed girls molested, incest, marriage discord; many young and aged men also disclosed their sexual concerns".

So it came about that Dr. Mahinder C. Watsa was pointed towards his calling – that of sexuality education for the youth as well as adults; and counselling and therapy. He picked up the gauntlet thrown by society and went about forging a path where none existed before: sometimes, meeting a lot of resistance; but ultimately, winning the respect and adulation of a vast majority of people.

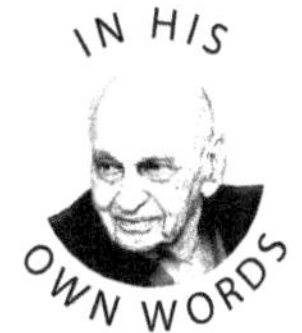

ADOLESCENTS HAVE RIGHTS -1

It is interesting to note that that even almost 50 years ago, Dr. Watsa, had such a clearsighted perspective - which may have been prevalent in western countries, but was not widely accepted here in India – as to accept that young persons have sexual rights. And he pioneered the dissemination of those rights in no uncertain terms to the target group.

Excerpts from Annexure I of Bloom and Blossom: Adolescent Guide to Growing Up. *A Publication of the Family Planning Association of India (FPAI):*

YOUNG PEOPLES' SEXUAL RIGHTS ARE HUMAN RIGHTS

Sexual rights are human rights and apply to everyone no matter what age. The 10 core sexual rights outlined in the Declaration all relate to young people. Each right is equally important, so the order in which they appear does not reflect any hierarchy of importance.

1. **The right to equality**

   All human beings are born free and equal in dignity and rights. Therefore, all young people should be able to exercise and fulfil their rights equally, including sexual rights. No young person should be discriminated against on the basis of sexuality, sex, gender, gender identity, sexual orientation, age, religion, race, ethnicity, nationality, HIV status, marital status, physical or mental disability, socio-economic status, or any other status. Barriers must be removed so that everyone, especially marginalised and under-served groups, can enjoy all human rights. Non-

discrimination is at the heart of promoting and protecting human rights.

2. **The right to participation**

   Everyone has the right to actively and freely participate in all aspects of human life. All young people are political beings. This means that all young people, including those under the age of majority, married and unmarried young people, young people living with HIV, young people living with disabilities, young migrants and young people of all sexual orientations and gender identities have the right to meaningfully participate in decision making that affects their lives and to influence changes in their societies.

3. **The right to life and to be free from harm**

   Everyone has the right to life, liberty and to be free from harm. This includes the right to express one's sexuality and gender free from coercion or violence. No one can be harassed, harmed, punished or killed because of their sexual practices, gender identity or expression, nor as a way to protect the reputation or honour of a family or community. Young unmarried women, YPLHIV, young lesbians, gay, bisexual, intersex and transgendered young people must be especially protected from harm and punishment. All children and young people must have special protection from all forms of exploitation and harm, especially sexual exploitation, child prostitution, trafficking, forced sexual activity, and being used in pornographic performances or materials. Harmful traditional practices, such as female genital mutilation, forced parenthood and child marriage, must be addressed to protect and fulfil all young people's sexual rights.

4. **The right to privacy**

   All young people have the right to privacy and to make autonomous decisions about their sexuality privately. All young people also have the right to decide if, when, how and with whom to share information about their sexual choices without forceful interference from other people.

5. **The right to personal autonomy and to be recognised as an individual before the law**

   All young people have the right to decide freely on all matters related to their sexuality and to fully experience their sexuality and gender in a pleasurable way. Everyone has the right to do so while being recognised as an individual before the law. Sexual rights can only be limited by laws in democratic societies that must be introduced to ensure the general public's welfare or health, or in order to protect people's rights and freedoms. Any limitation on sexual rights must be non discriminatory, including on the grounds of age.

6. **The right to think and express oneself freely**

   All young people have the right to express their thoughts, opinions, needs and desires related to sexuality without limitations based on dominant cultural beliefs or political ideologies. All young people have the right to explore their sexualities and should be able to have dreams and fantasies, and voluntarily express their sexuality without fear, shame or guilt, while respecting other people's rights. This should occur in a non-discriminatory environment that respects the evolving capacities of young people.

7. **The right to health**

   Every young person has the right to enjoy the highest attainable standard of physical and mental health and well-being, including sexual and reproductive health and the underlying factors that contribute to health. Young

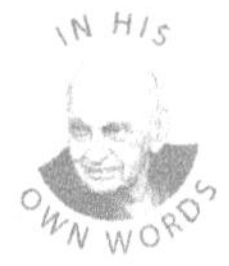

people also have the right to be protected from social, environmental and economic factors that lead to poor health status.

8. **The right to know and learn**

   All young people have the right to education and information, including comprehensive, gender-sensitive and rights-based sexuality education. All young people have the right to access accurate, easy to understand information and education about sexuality, sexual health, reproductive health, sexual rights and reproductive rights in order to make decisions freely and with informed consent.

9. **The right to choose whether or not to marry or have children**

   Every young person has the right to choose when, if, how and whom to marry and have children in an environment that recognizes diverse family types.

10. **The right to have your rights upheld**

    Governments must respect, protect and fulfil all sexual rights for young people. Respect means not interfering directly or indirectly with young people's enjoyment of their rights. Protect means taking measures to prevent others from interfering with young people's human rights. Fulfil means adopting laws, policies and programmes that enable young people to fully realise their sexual rights.

    While governments have the main responsibility to ensure rights, civil society also plays an important role. Many leaders, institutions and stakeholders influence people's ability to exercise their rights and are therefore responsible for upholding people's rights. Every young person is entitled to hold their leaders accountable to their commitments and responsibilities to uphold sexual rights.

All young people must have access to legal or judicial procedures in case any of their rights are violated. States must put mechanisms into place that positively protect, respect and fulfil rights, as well as mechanisms that discourage violations from happening in the first place. States should ensure that sexual rights violators are brought to justice.

CHAPTER 6

THE WIND BENEATH HIS WINGS

1970s

A little bit of the sheen which had enveloped the New World since the end of WW II, had worn out by the time the decade of the 1970s dawned. It was a period of mixed happenings and mixed emotions.

Perhaps more significant were the dark clouds gathering on the economic front, after a fairly long period of prosperity. And wars, conflicts and coups dotted the landscape across the globe.

Yet, it was also a decade which saw "great technological and scientific advances". It marked the onset of the "portability and home accessibility" of computing units, which have since evolved beyond all recognition of the initial unwieldy machines tethered to the ground.

India continued to grapple with poverty and all the social ills related to it. The worsening economic situation was sharpened by the famine in the eastern part of the country which had struck in the previous decade. Within the country, one of the key events of the 1970s was the Emergency.

Among the different aspects of the Emergency that were later criticised was the manner in which the family planning programme was implemented, where thousands of unsuspecting men and women were forced to undergo sterilisation operations to 'meet targets'.

Here, it is important to emphasise that this has nothing to do with the topic of this book and characters within it as their concept of family planning using contraceptive methods was aimed at giving more control to women (and men) over their own bodies – not to take it away from them. The 'nas bandi' *campaign as it was popularly known has been mentioned just to recall the historical context and applaud the distinctly different approach of the protagonist of this book.*

All in all, the Seventies was a decade which historians have described as "the pivot of change". And that it certainly was, in more ways than one, both at an international and national level.

> "You see things; and you say, 'Why?' But I dream things that never were; and I say, 'Why not?'"
>
> **George Bernard Shaw**
> *Playwright, Critic & Political Activist*

The year 1973 marked a nodal milestone in the journey of our intrepid traveller. Nodal because all the roads traversed so far, the various streams of his life seemed to converge at this point from where he took off on a consolidated new journey; the year marking, in Dr. Mahinder Watsa's own words, "the start of the fulfilment of his aspirations". It was the year as he highlighted, when he switched his practice exclusively to what he himself defined as a "sex educator, counsellor and therapist", with a mission "to have sexuality recognised as an ethical speciality", he had said.

It was, crucially, also the year Dr. Watsa joined the Family Planning Association of India (FPAI), which proved to be a fitting vehicle to propel him towards the fulfilment of his dreams and goals.

Even today, long after he had stopped being actively involved in the organisation, it is as if his name is emblazoned in neon letters in the annals of that organisation's history.

"We at the FPAI respect him greatly," enthuses Dr. Kalpana Apte, the current Secretary General of the organisation. "He is held in great love and esteem by all of us, and his passing was a personal loss to me."

Though Dr. Apte is much younger than Dr. Watsa, he was still associated with the FPAI when she joined around the 1990s, fresh from medical college; and she had had the opportunity to work closely with him.

Dr. Watsa was introduced to the FPAI through his old friend, and by then close associate Dr. Rusi Soonawala. The latter had been appointed on the International Planned Parenthood Federation (IPPF) and had also joined FPAI as a Medical Director in 1965. Since then, the working interaction between Dr. Rusi Soonawala and Dr. Watsa had increased significantly.

"With all my work outside my practice, there were times when I was unable to look after my patients," recalls Dr. Soonawala. "So that they would not be, and feel, neglected, Dr. Watsa and I joined hands. If I was unavailable, he would be there to see my patients." This arrangement continued for a while, as long as the need for it existed.

Considering Dr. Watsa's growing interest in immersing himself once again completely in medical practice – specifically that of social medicine – and in withdrawing from his corporate role, it was only a matter of time before Dr. Soonawala introduced Dr. Watsa to the then President of the FPAI, Mrs. Avabai Wadia. Shortly thereafter, having resigned from Glaxo, Dr. Mahinder C. Watsa joined the FPAI, as a consultant on medical affairs.

The Family Planning Association of India was set up in 1949 by two very talented, capable, women achievers: Lady Dhanvanthi Rama Rau and Avabai Wadia. They belonged to an earlier era and were amongst the galaxy of women who were educated, forward thinking and dedicated to the progress of their country and welfare of society in general; and that of women in particular.

The former, born in 1893, was one of the first women in the country to attend college and went on to teach English at Queen Mary's College in Madras between 1917–21. A founding member, she was active with the FPAI from its inception in 1949 up to 1963; and went on to serve as the President of the International Planned Parenthood Federation from 1963 to 1971.

Avabai Wadia, Lady Dhanvanthi's junior by several years, was born on September 18, 1913 in Colombo, British Ceylon (Sri Lanka), into what has been described as "an affluent and highly westernised Parsi family with roots in Gujarat, India".

She was sent to England, accompanied by her mother, at the age of 15 years to complete her schooling; and later joined the Inns of Court to become a lawyer, to which she had aspired since the age of 13 years. Soon, she had the distinction of being the first Ceylonese woman to become a lawyer. She was also perhaps the youngest woman in those times to qualify as one, at the age of 19 years.

In Britain, in the early years of the 20th century, the women of that country had begun the struggle to attain equality. Theirs was an ever-swelling cry and one taken up by other nationalities which had gravitated to the land from different parts of the world, as well.

Avabai had felt the tug to contribute to society at a fairly young age – even when she was in school and later studying the law – "the notions of social justice were becoming embedded in me", she says in her magnificent and detailed book, *The Light is Ours: Memoirs & Movements.*

She was only 16 years when she was invited to join the London Committee of the Women's India Association – where, in fact, she met up with Dhanvanthi Rama Rau, with whom she was later to team up.

In her own memoirs, Avabai explains her journey towards what was to become her lasting passion and dedication.

"It was through my work as editor of the AIWC (ed: All-India Women's Conference) monthly magazine *Roshni* that my contact with family planning work, which eventually led to a lifelong interest and involvement in this field began," she writes. "The women's movement was still very concerned with the poor health of women, which was partly caused by their having too many children too frequently and therefore some of the women's organisations were interested in introducing birth control services. However, they had very little guidance on how to do it, and almost no funds."

Though a first step had been taken in Mumbai when a couple of centres were set up by the then Bombay Municipal Council (BMC) and one by a woman's organisation, Avabai recounts that most women in those days "had not even heard of family planning, nor were they aware of the existence of the centres".

That is when she and her associates decided to try and popularise the concept. "Mrs. E. Vembu a social worker, who had been contributing occasional articles to newspapers, approached me to discuss publicising family planning through articles in *Roshni*. I agreed, but we realised that we could not reach underprivileged and largely illiterate mothers in this way. As a result, we got together a group of experienced social workers and medical practitioners, both men and women, and formed the Family Planning Committee, which soon became the Family Planning Association in India."

And so it was that the organisation, which was to play such a significant role in Dr. Watsa's life, was born in 1949. The goal then, and therefore even the mandate, was to be able to restore to women some degree of control and decision making over their own bodies and reproductive health and planning.

Earlier, some two decades previously, Avabai herself had been beset with doubts and questions regarding "birth control" – especially since she first heard of the concept at a public meeting where the speaker had made some very racist remarks in conjunction with the need for controlling the population.

It was when she read the transcript of a speech delivered by Dr. Lakshmi Joshi (who later married Major General C.R. Rajwade), who said that Indian women were fated to live a life that "oscillated between gestation and lactation until death wound up the sorry tale", that she was "deeply affected" she recalled.

"It was in trying to understand the lives of women and the compulsion I felt to work for their welfare and rights, that I came to believe in the need, significance and wisdom of controlling conception, so that every child was a wanted child and mothers were at the same time women in their own right," Avabai says in her memoirs.

Before we take up the thread of Dr. Watsa's story, there was another development in earlier history that is connected to him and his future work. That was the formation of the International Planned Parenthood Federation (IPPF) with which, too, he was to become intimately involved; and through which he did a lot of his work. What is more, the prominent members of this organisation, representing different countries, were people with whom he collaborated to spread his mission and launch new fora. The IPPF continues to be the apex body of all national bodies advocating and working for sexual and reproductive health and the rights of the individual with regard to them in various countries.

It was in 1952, that an event took place in India, which was to be a significant one in the family planning saga of the country. This was the organisation of the Third International Conference on Planned Parenthood. The lead was taken by Margaret Sanger (an eminent American feminist, widely seen as the founder of the 'birth control' movement – and even credited with coining the term, apparently).

Avabai Wadia was one of a group of younger members of the FPAI who were entrusted with the actual task of organising the event.

It was an extremely successful conference with representation from various countries which had existing associations for planned parenthood. In fact, the impassioned cry of a Japanese delegate and proponent of family planning who said "You have no idea how many lives you will be able to save!" has echoed down the decades and the truth of his words has been an inspiration propelling the army of workers, whether medical professionals or others, who worked for sexual and reproductive health.

At the conclusion of its proceedings, the conference passed a formal resolution to transform the International Committee for Planned Parenthood into a federation. Countries where such associations didn't yet exist were invited to join as Associate Members. Thus, the International Planned Parenthood Federation (IPPF) came into being on November 29, 1952.

Taking up the threads of our story once again, we find that by the time Dr. Mahinder C. Watsa joined the FPAI in 1973, Avabai was in, so to say, "sole" charge of the body with Lady Dhanvanthi having moved on to become President of the IPPF in 1963.

Avabai not only served as Secretary General and two terms as President of the organisation (both posts spanning several decades), but in later years was honoured with the titles of President Emeritus and Patron.

The FPAI proved to be a perfect fit for Dr. Watsa, and vice versa. His own forward looking, forward thinking, liberal nature both, resonated with, and revelled in, the achievements of the ladies who had founded the organisation and contributed so much to women and children's welfare, to which he himself was wholly committed.

By now, Dr. Watsa had come to the conclusion, based on his decades of interaction with women and children as a doctor, as well as all the problems brought to him by readers through his column in *Trend* and then in *Femina*, that sexuality education was – of both adolescents and adults – was of utmost importance for the overall sexual well-being of individuals and society. He had realised that there was not only a lack of knowledge but, in its absence, misinformation and misconceptions predominated people's consciousness, confounding matters further.

Looking back on these years in the course of compiling his Curriculum Vitae he describes (in the third person) how his clinical practice had opened his eyes to these issues, and his interaction with people writing in to him for his columns further sharpened his perspective, saying: "….as a regular author of the '*Doctor Talks to You*' page in the *Femina* magazine for more than 15 years he learnt much about the undercurrent of sexuality prevalent among all levels of Indian society.

"He (ed: Dr. Watsa) was frustrated to learn, that neither was sexuality considered an ethical subject and doctors knew little of the subject nor were there any social organisations or persons that the distressed could turn to. There was no structured course on marriage counselling and therapy for sexual problems. Therefore, during his studies in the U.K. and later in 1973 he frequently visited the marriage guidance bureau (later known as 'Relate') in the U.K. He was concerned that behind the majority of marriage conflicts there was a sexual problem. He also observed the changing sexual behaviour over the years, particularly of young people. Incest, child molestation, the silence of rape and domestic violence; the depression of impotency and confusion in homosexuality became more and more evident."

As he said above, and at different times, the issues were widespread and may have different nuances across age, gender and demographic segments, but at the basis there was some commonality too – namely, problems of sexuality and a lack of scientific information on one hand; and on the other the prevalence of social taboos and myths obfuscating the question of sexuality, sexual desire, even sexual identity.

Surprisingly, the issues, questions and misconceptions surrounding sexuality had remained almost the same through the decades that Dr. Watsa was professionally active – which was almost to the end of his life – a period covering almost 70 years!

"One of the common problems we saw, was non-consummation of marriages for a period of time varying from seven days to two years or more, during which time couples had not experienced proper penetrative sexual intercourse," observes Dr. Shirish Malde.

Further, there are issues of erectile dysfunction: these could be due to a medical condition or due to mental health issues. Sometimes it can even be a bit of a chicken and egg question, Dr. Malde feels.

"Many couples may be suffering from chronic sexual problems and they may not even be aware of it," reveals Dr. Malde. "It may manifest itself in irritability. Others are hyperactive, more aggressive; sometimes exactly the opposite. Sometimes the problem starts with psychological mood swings."

"On the other hand," Dr. Malde continues, "sexual anxiety amongst the young mainly pertains to masturbation, penis size, nocturnal ejaculation, hair growth, low count of male hormones; sometimes they are worried about their orientation – for example, someone might get an erection when they come in contact with another man, say on a train."

Dr. Watsa recognised that there was too, the danger of younger girls and boys falling prey to sexual predators due to sheer lack of awareness and knowledge about their bodies. Then, there were the adolescents and teenagers who just didn't know how to cope with their burgeoning bodies and growing sexual needs and desires.

All sorts of myths and irrational and superstitious beliefs persisted as, in most cases, there was no scientific discussion at home, or in schools and colleges; indeed, often there was no discussion at all, and the sheer conservatism of parents and teachers made them fairly unapproachable.

One area, particularly, that was little addressed was that of sexual identity. Youngsters who experienced feelings for the same sex, or who were not comfortable with the gender assigned to them at birth, found there was no way they could express their feelings and thoughts.

Former journalist and the first gay rights activist of India, Ashok Row Kavi, (now a senior citizen) who himself came out several decades ago, lived in an adjacent building to that in which the Watsa home was, at Shivaji Park, Mumbai. The two families were friends and there was much interaction and a close friendship between Dr. Watsa and Ashok from the earliest days till the fateful lockdown during the course of which Dr. Watsa passed away.

Questions and issues surrounding sexual and reproductive health in general and homosexuality in particular, were often discussed between them, which, possibly helped Dr. Watsa gain an insight into and understanding of this area of concern.

"Dr Watsa was a very open person," recalls Ashok Row Kavi with a hint of sadness. "One of the greatest things about him was that when there were things he didn't understand, he was always willing to discuss and listen to another point of view. I miss people like him."

Ashok remembers that their talks about homosexuality – from the time he became old enough, and clear enough in his views, to engage in discussion – ranged from incredulity, to wondering what could be done to rectify the "propensity" to understanding, support and engagement.

"He would say initially that he had heard of homosexuality and read about it but not met many people who are gay and he was willing to try and understand them," says Ashok. "As he delved into understanding the gay world, he tried to untie various knots and he got more and more sympathetic, but he also got very worried. You see a lot of gay men are in self-exile. They feel marginalised, criminalised and the mind turns onto itself. Then, there are a lot of people who don't accept you or like you. Coming to accept yourself for who you are with all the various currents a gay person faces is very difficult."

Though, in a sense, a lot of progress has been made when it comes to accepting gay relationships, there are still sections of society which are not accepting of gay persons and others of the LGBTQ community.

From the early days of his sexuality practice, Dr. Watsa took care to draw out persons who might have gender identity issues and provide them with the counselling essential for them.

In later years, when he felt that it would help the individual to understand and adjust better, he would also introduce them to Ashok, who had by then started the Hamsafar Trust and become one of India's first activists to campaign for LGBTQ rights.

People had nowhere to take their queries and problems; and no one to ask for information. As a result, genuine questions instead of being addressed to qualified doctors, were being taken to quacks who had neither the knowledge nor the inclination to sort out issues thrown up; they only wanted to make a fast buck.

Also, Dr. Watsa had observed that even a vast number of doctors were ill informed about matters of sexuality and family planning as well.

FPAI's self definition and mission and vision statements all seem to have expanded since the time when it was first formed. Initially, the emphasis was on family planning, as in birth control, with regards to the health of the woman and child.

Today, the words "sexual and reproductive health" have come to define the organisation and have taken on an increasing focus since the last several decades. While it may be reflective of the progress and developments on the wider canvas as well as international wisdom in the field, that is only part of the story. There can be no doubt that it is the clear-sighted vision and its strenuous practical application of people like Dr. Watsa, which have helped the organisation to take on a more holistic approach and role.

Though the focus of his mission was sharpened when he joined the FPAI, by no way did it pop up out of the blue, without context or background.

As Dr. Soonawala pointed out, even before he set out to do all that he did at FPAI, and before he formally set up as a Sex Counsellor and Therapist, Dr. Watsa was already advising people who had any kind of marital or sexual problems. "He would guide couples on how to get along, that was how he eventually started sexuality education," Dr. Soonawala emphasises. "His efforts were so sincere and the need for what he was doing was great; especially as sex was a taboo field, that to break through that prejudice needed great conviction."

By the early 1970s, Dr. Mahinder C. Watsa, in order to fulfil his avowed goal, had obtained yet another qualification – he had become a Certified Sex Educator and Counsellor by qualifying through AASECT (USA). The American Association of Sexuality Educators, Counsellors and Therapists (AASECT) was, and remains, one the most authentic certifying bodies for such a practice. From then on, Dr. Watsa had decided to focus his practice on the subject of sexual and reproductive health, though the term may not yet have gained coinage.

(As an aside, and on a lighter note, there is this amusing incident recounted by Dr. Watsa's daughter-in-law Deepa Watsa; to whom the story was narrated first hand by the doctor himself. When he decided to change his practice and concentrate wholly on sexology, he needed a new signboard for his clinic which was duly ordered. The genius painter brought back the painted signboard, which read "Sex Counselor and The rapist" instead of "Sex Counselor and Therapist" – much to Dr. Watsa's amusement, and also consternation. And if you have heard of this one before, now you know the origin of this little contretemps!)

Soon after Dr. Watsa joined the FPAI, he presented his views on the issue of sexuality and the lack of knowledge surrounding it, to Avabai, who was then President of the FPAI. He told her that it was a subject about which little was known and still less understood, strongly advocating for the need for sexuality education. He urged that education, particularly of adolescents, be taken up by holding sex education lecture-workshops at various places. Avabai, recognising the wisdom of his words, readily assented, and thereon began one of the quietest, yet amongst the more significant revolutions, on the country's social landscape.

Dr. Watsa described Avabai as "a person of great vision and foresight who boldly backed (him)… to introduce the sensitive subject of sexuality into FPAIndia's activities."

Not one to let the grass grow under his feet, in the year following his joining, Dr. Watsa convened a meet, "Tomorrow's Parents Today"; a conference he described as "for young people and by young people". Looking back, he had remarked, "Thus, the FPAI became the first in the country to recognise the adolescents' role in reproductive and sexual health."

One far-reaching early achievement was when Dr. Watsa – with Avabai's assent – went on to establish the FPAI SECRT. This refers to the Sex Education Counselling Research Training/Therapy Project under which centres were set up across the country in various cities and towns.

These became not only a place from where sexuality education could be carried out, but also a beacon for adolescents in times of distress, to which they could reach out for information and support. The SECRT centres were a valuable resource for the organisation and remained operational for several decades.

Dr. Watsa explained later, that he chose to focus "on sexual education and counselling for better reproductive and sexual health".

"Dr. Watsa believed in counselling and sex therapy," Dr. Reddy elaborates upon the approach of his long time colleague and friend. "Today, doctors have only become penis-centric and dependent on medicine, pharma, focussing on the physical; and the psychogenic aspects do not get much emphasis."

This approach has very definite implications. Dr. Reddy explains, saying, "This means the doctor doesn't have to find out the exact cause of the problem – the relationship issues responsible for the problem. Dr. Watsa believed we should take this up hand in hand along with medicine – so he believed that counselling and therapy were extremely important."

According to him, men focus on erection; while women's concerns are more about lack of desire and lack of orgasms. "I have been in practice for over 39 years," says Dr. Reddy elaborating on the insights he has gained. "I always tell my clients spend time together, understand each other's feelings, indulge in foreplay, open up and talk, instil confidence in each other. But, whether they are interested in relationships or performance, there are lot of misconceptions."

These could very well have been the words of Dr. Watsa, for they both shared the same approach and philosophy towards sexual health.

One can imagine that this was said with the belief that prevention is better than cure – at least for those affected – and that matters should not be allowed to slide to the extent that the relationship was difficult to save.

Malathi Pillai who worked with Dr. Watsa in the area of counselling when she was in the FPAI thinks back on her experience then. He was counselling not only married couples but also pre-marriage couples and adolescents.

"Looking back one can say that many of the problems brought to him in his counselling/therapy practice then, were similar to those he tackled in his columns," she remarks. "A young boy might have night falls, or face guilt about masturbation and so on."

Malathi recalls that Dr. Watsa was very open. "He always reassured the young people there was nothing to be ashamed of and there was nothing amiss," she says.

It was all about de-mystifying sex and removing the myths and misconceptions surrounding it, Malathi remembers. "And that is the approach he imparted to everyone, and upon which he built the organisation – he stressed that there was nothing demeaning about sex; that sex was not a 'four letter word'," she emphasises.

Malathi gives the example of one case which is not only reflective of the efficacy of Dr. Watsa's approach, but also an example of the kind of team he built up. "From my own experience, I can say how people were helped," she begins. "One of the persons working with me in those days got married, and his wife had not conceived even after a bit of time had elapsed. So I sent them to the FPAI to get checked up. Soon after, his wife became pregnant. It was not Dr. Watsa who treated them but it was the entire organisation which he had created, which could tackle all problems!" Dr. Watsa's work was holistic. Even with the FPAI, it was not merely about contraception or birth control – it was about the entire spectrum of sexual and reproductive health from the outset.

The inability to conceive was a fairly common problem faced by young couples, as Dr. Watsa and his colleagues found. They encountered several cases where the couple had not been able to conceive and were concerned there was something wrong with one or the other of them; but the problem turned out to be that they had not even consummated the marriage. As one of his colleagues echoes views aired before, "Those were the days mainly of arranged marriages. He had no clue, and she had no clue about what to do. Couples who had not consummated their marriages after weeks, and sometimes for several months even, would often come to us."

The doctors and sexologists then had to impart information of the male and female body with the help of charts and even with actual models of male and female genitals when they became available.

Just as adult couples benefitted from instruction and were able to go on to properly consummate their marriages, and, in the majority of case, also to conceive; with adolescents it helped in alerting them about good touch/bad touch and what to beware of and what to absolutely not allow.

However, consummation and conception were only one set of problems. There were others too.

Malathi touches upon an aspect, which also highlights another facet of Dr. Watsa's outlook. "One male chauvinist belief is that if there is a problem about consummating a marriage it is because of the woman – because she is frigid," she recounts. "I remember once we had gone to Kerala for a seminar for college students and one of the people there asked: 'What do you do when Indian women are frigid?' Dr. Watsa replied – 'Maybe the problem is that Indian men do not know how to arouse women?' And that says it all!"

Deepa Watsa remembers that the road was not always smooth, and there were many people who would pass snide remarks or would attack him downright. "Dad once told me about an incident, going way back," she narrates. "He was in Chennai and speaking to the Mental Hygiene Association of India. They stopped him in the middle of the talk and said 'What is this pornographic material you are talking about?' Dr. Watsa very calmly told the audience if they didn't want to hear him speak, it was fine by him. Soon a large commotion ensued in the hall as some wanted to hear his talk and some didn't. It so happened that a girl from Loyola College who was one of the secretaries of the students' body, stood up and said 'What are you all talking about? Let me take you to the beach (in Chennai) and show you the couples who are having sex there. I will take you to the abortion centers as well'. She gave them hell. The crowd then realised all that had been going on and which was being swept under the carpet. Finally, calm was restored and everyone said 'We would really like to hear you, Dr. Watsa'."

It did not take Dr. Watsa long to get into his stride after he joined the FPAI. Soon he began holding lectures, seminars, workshops at educational institutions and other places across the country; as well as in neighbouring countries like Pakistan, Bangladesh, Nepal, Sri Lanka – and even in Cyprus and Egypt.

On the other hand, he began attending workshops, meetings and conferences in different countries like the Philippines, Italy, UK and the USA, as a result of which he greatly "developed his knowledge", Dr. Watsa himself had remarked.

Early in the day, he had also realised that most doctors themselves did not have the knowledge, nor the counselling skill or the approach to deal with sexual problems. Hence, lectures and workshops for medical personnel were included on his agenda too.

Dr. Ruby Baam, who had joined the FPAI in 1975 and began working with Dr. Watsa's department towards the end of that decade, recalls how her role underwent a total transformation as Dr. Watsa put her in charge of the task of organising training programmes for the medical fraternity. This was yet another characteristic of the doctor – his encouragement to those working with him to undertake new roles and to support them to the fullest.

"Each programme would depend on the group – sometimes we held a conference for doctors, sometimes for post graduate medical students – those who had done their MD/MS, and then for other segments of the medical profession," she recalls. "We organised both theory and practical sessions. Doctors and students would come from all over India – and even from Pakistan, Sri Lanka, Bangladesh."

Programmes were also organised for pharmacists and nurses as well as for general practitioners including not only the MBBS doctors, but also those practising alternative systems of medicine like homoeopathy, ayurveda, and unani.

"Under Dr. Watsa we ran several programmes: sex education training centres, counselling – if there was discord in marriages or if couples faced sexual problems," recalls Dr. Baam. "We also organised programmes for adolescents – Dr. Watsa was very keen on imparting sex education and training to the younger generation."

While it would be impossible to cover all the seminars, workshops and conferences he organised over the several decades of his professional life at FPAI, one stands out as an important marker; the flag-off for establishing an army of sexology practitioners and educators that he went on to build.

The milestone workshop – with Dr. M. C. Watsa listed as the Chief Organiser – on '*Human Sexuality in Family Life*', convened under the auspices of the FPAI was the first such to be organised in the country, although similar-themed workshops had been held by WHO in Geneva and Manila.

For this workshop, the IPPF extended invaluable support in the way of sponsoring the services of two resource persons: Dr. Vicente Rosales, as an expert Consultant to the workshop; and Dr. Raymundo Rivera, Training Officer IPPF, London, who had also attended the WHO workshop in Geneva in 1974.

While the pinpointing of topics, resource persons and speakers seems to have been fairly uncomplicated, the process of choosing participants was more complex. Strict criteria were laid down, and the initial announcement of the planned workshop was circulated to governmental and about 100 non-governmental agencies and the FPAI branches, seeking applications. Once these organisations reverted, with individuals expressing interest, each applicant was sent a form with detailed bio-data requirements to be filled in. Every form received back was scrutinised to ensure just the right mix of knowledge, skills and experience were represented to fit into the objectives of the workshop.

Dr. Saroj Jha remembers that Dr. Watsa made it a point to include people from different persuasions – doctors, nurses, social workers, people from the media etc.

The programme of the workshop held in Pune, Maharashtra, from February 26 to March 3, 1977, underwent similar attention and careful crafting, with Dr. Prakash Kothari and Mrs. Dorothy Bapat participating in the process of preparing the initial draft. It had inputs from Dr. Sarah Israel; it was checked for practicality by Dr. Rivera to ensure that that it would run smoothly; and was finally vetted by Dr. Rosales himself.

Dr. Watsa believed that this first ever residential workshop on human sexuality in Asia to be of particular significance. It was organised he said, with a view "to open the minds of the health professionals, social workers, and the media to its importance". He further summed up the significance of the landmark event saying: "The workshop was memorable as it proved to be the cornerstone of the start of ethical sexuality in India. Many of those who attended have become expert resource persons and are recognised as authorities on sexuality education counselling and therapy."

Those who participated in the workshop, still remember it for the first-ever candid discussion on sex and sexuality.

Ashok Row Kavi, who was one of the participants, remembers how Dr. Watsa defended his presentation on issues related to homosexuality, which were looked at askance by many, including the then head of FPAI, Dr. Avabai Wadia, according to him. Ashok recalls that her position was that there is "no connection between homosexuality and reproductive issues".

However, Dr. Watsa put forward the opinion that homosexuality was possibly a deviation or a variation; and not a perversion. "This was heard by the mostly conservative audience and agreed to in the final report," Ashok recalls.

The discussions over those five-six days were wide-ranging; and the conference had the participation of some of the leading counsellors and social activists, who had been chosen after much vetting. But despite the fact that the participants were all stalwarts in their fields, the sessions must have been, and according to all reports were, quite an eye-opener for all.

That Conference marked the first step of an extremely important journey.

"The whole development of sex education was to the credit of Dr. Watsa," stresses Dr. Soonawala. "It was an education which was a necessity, absolutely essential. He removed the taboo, so people could feel free to voice their concerns. His charming manner and ability to break barriers opened the public's mind to the fact that sex is not something dirty and not to be discussed at all. In my opinion this would probably be one of his greatest and everlasting contributions to Indian society."

There were other initiatives which Dr. Watsa introduced as well; and though launched in the late 1970s, those actually took off in the following decades and hence are elaborated upon in the next chapter.

In the decade of the 1970s, at the age of almost 50 years, Dr. Watsa spread his wings, and soared off in a new direction, showing the way for many who came after him, indeed for many of his contemporaries as well.

A SCIENTIFIC APPROACH

In the course of his work with the FPAI, Dr. Mahinder Watsa conducted several studies and mapped the issues, knowledge and information lacuna at different times and with varied focus points. Sometimes, studies were carried out with organisations like Tata Institute of Social Sciences (TISS), and sometimes with their own internal resources. Once more, what comes to the fore is his scientific approach and his continuous endeavour to conduct his work with a strong foundation of just that.

Reproduced below are glimpses from one such survey in the mid 1990s, when HIV and AIDS emerged as a major health concern.

YOUTH SEXUALITY

PREFACE

Family Planning Association of India, Sex Education, Counselling, Research, Therapy and Training (FPAI-SECRT) Department (study), undertaken in 1994, complements the 1990 study - *Attitudes and Perceptions of Educated Urban Youth to Marriage and Sex.* More than four thousand respondents from the North, South, East and West zones have been interviewed to assess the knowledge, attitudes, values, beliefs and practices about sexuality. Particular attention has been paid to assessing sexually transmitted diseases (STDs) and HIV/AIDS.

A study of this type could only be undertaken firmly keeping in mind the milieu and sensitivity of the people. The formulation of the questionnaire took more than a year, passing through several expert hands knowledgeable about the subject or the research methodology to be utilised. A pre-test at five centres gave confidence to the persons administering the questionnaire that the nature of the questions would not offend. Young people, in fact, were eager to answer and help in getting their friends to answer. The experience gained by the staff in the previous large survey helped to avoid repetition of the errors. Before the survey was launched all the investigators underwent a familiarisation programme. A common strategy to be followed at all Centres was devised. The questionnaire which was in English was translated into the respective investigator's language so that the questions could be understood by all respondents. Interesting data has emerged which will help health professionals to formulate the strategies and plan of action. Also it will clear a number of misconceptions and beliefs about the sexuality of the young people.

No survey can be completed without support. The unstinted backing and understanding of the President, Mrs Avabai B Wadia, is recognised. The permission to conduct the survey by the Secretary General Air Vice Marshal (Retd.) ES Lala is appreciated. The survey has been wholly funded by the FPAI. Without the enthusiastic support and hard work of the Counsellors/Consultants of SECRT, the Research and Evaluation Department of FPAI specially Ms Armin Jamshedji in the analysis and coding aspects (this study could not have been completed). Dr Ravi Verma of the International Institute of Population Sciences and Ms. Manisha Shah have meticulously worked in making this survey accurate.

Mahinder C. Watsa
Consultant (Former), SECRT

INTRODUCTION:

There has been a sudden surge of interest mainly with the advent of AIDS in studying matters related to sex and sexuality, during the last decade. Small scale qualitative as well as quantitative studies have been conducted in this area. Most of this research has been on high risk groups such as commercial sex workers and homosexuals. Very few large scale studies were conducted, which were mainly through national magazines. In 1990, one large scale study covering 3,846 respondents was conducted by FPAI-SECRT on attitudes and perceptions of educated, urban youth to marriage and sex. Therefore, there is very little documented information available about the early experiences, attitudes, and opinions on sex and sexuality among youth in India.

Indian youth, in the absence of systematic and correct information on matters related to sex and sexuality, are facing a dilemma between traditional Indian norms and western patterns of expression. A recently conducted study in Pune found that 75% of those attending a Sexually Transmitted Disease (STD) clinic were between 18-19 years[1]. With changing lifestyles, youth often experiment in the process of discovering their sexuality and are more likely to have unprotected sexual intercourse with a greater risk of contacting an STD or having an unwanted pregnancy. Under these changing circumstances, the introduction of effective sex education programmes for all levels of society, particularly for school and out-of-school children is becoming increasingly relevant. There is an urgent need for policy makers, programme planners and implementors of sex education programmes to understand the greater proportion of the population who are young and who are not "high risk".

[1] A C Urmil, P K Dutta, S S Ganguly. Medico-social profile of male teenager STD patients attending a clinic in Pune. Indian Journal of Public Health, 33 (4): 176-82, Oct-Dec 1989.

Recognising this lacuna, FPAI-SECRT conducted the present study on sexuality and patterns of sexual behaviour among urban youth representing the four zones of India. This was after a period of three years of the first survey in 1990. The primary objectives of this study were to:

- assess the knowledge, source of information, attitudes, opinions and practice among youth on human reproduction, sexuality, STD/HIV(AIDS), and family planning, and
- identify differences among male and female urban youth in the four zones of the country.

*****

Correct Knowledge About Prevention of STD Infection:

Knowledge of preventing an STD infection is a prerequisite for ensuring a healthy sexual and reproductive life especially for youth. Thus, the respondents' level of knowledge on prevention of STD/AIDS was assessed through this survey. This analysis revealed that in all the age groups in all the Zones, except North, a higher proportion of the males than females gave the correct response of preventing an STD by the **use of condoms**. This difference was two times more for respondents between 15-19 years and 20-23 years in the North and South Zones, while it was three times more in the East Zone. Between the age groups 20-23 and 24-29 years the difference was minimised. While there was an increase in the number of male respondents giving this response with increase in age in the East Zone, and female respondents from the North and South Zones, there was a decline among males in the North and South Zones and among females in the West Zone. A higher percent of the respondents from the West Zone and a lower percent from the South gave this response

than in the other Zones. A significantly higher percent of male (60.3%) than female (36.3%) gave this response.

There was a decline in the number of male respondents stating **sexual abstinence** as a method of preventing an STD infection with increase in age, except for male respondents in the East Zone. This was also true of female respondents in the North Zone. A higher percent of female respondents in the age group 20-24 in the East (33.6%), West (15.7%) and South (12.3%) Zone stated this than in the other age groups. A higher percent of the respondents from the West Zone and a lower percent from the South Zone gave this response than respondents from the other Zones. Only 16.4% and 13.1% male and female respondents, respectively, gave this response.

While there was an increase with increase in age among male respondents in the East, West and South Zones and among female respondents in the East, North, and South Zones, there was a decline among males in the North Zone who stated that STD infection can be prevented by **avoiding sex with strangers.** Again, except for the North Zone, a higher percent of males than females gave this response. Twice as many male than female respondents in the East Zone gave this response. Respondents from the West Zone gave this response more frequently and least from the East Zone than respondents from the other Zones. Nearly sixty percent of the male respondents and 42.3% female respondents stated avoiding sex with strangers as preventing an STD infection.

Not having multiple sex partners as another way of preventing an STD infection was stated more frequently by male respondents in all the age groups in the East and West Zone, and among adolescents in the North and South Zones. This was stated more frequently by females in age groups 20-23 and 24-29 years in the North Zone and those between

20-23 years in the South Zone. Respondents from the West Zone gave this response more frequently and least from the East Zone than those from the other zones. Over half (52.2%) male and 43.6% female respondents opined that not having multiple sex partners could prevent an STD infection.

Irrespective of age and zone, a higher percent of the male respondents stated that STD can be prevented by **washing genitals**. Females in their late adolescence in the East and North Zones had this misconception. Teenage females had the least response to this item. Less than a quarter of the respondents stated this as a preventive measure. A higher percent of teenage males than in females in all the zones stated **withdrawal method** as a way of preventing an STD. No significant male-female variation was found among respondents who were 20 and above years of age in all the zones. Overall, this response was given by 7.1% male and 3.4% female respondents.

CHAPTER 7

SPREADING THE WORD

1980s-1990s

The two decades, of the 1980s and 1990s, were watershed years; and a bridge from the 1970s – and decades immediately prior to it – to the new millennium.

In the US, the 1980s, dubbed the "Decade of Greed", saw the advent of neoliberal policies, or "free-market" economics; a philosophy and policy which were to spread to several other geographies the world over.

It was around this period, too, that gay persons began campaigning for their rights in the West; and while homosexual relations did become "acceptable" to some extent, "violence and a legal backlash against gay rights occurred throughout the decade", it has been reported.

In India, the seeds of economic liberalisation were sown in the 1980s. The 1990s marked a new beginning of growth and prosperity for the Indian economy with an increase in the pace and spread of economic liberalisation, *leading to the rise and burgeoning of a new aspirational middle class.*

Worldwide, these two decades witnessed technology taking a leap and the widespread use of "personal computers" and the birth and growth of the internet and its usage. The period marked the onset of globalisation, the telescoping of the world into a village and the interconnection between countries and their economies.

And whether you were in the Western, Eastern, Northern or Southern Hemisphere, one development which was to have a huge impact on the lives of most populations, was the launch of Google in 1998.

"Education is the most powerful weapon which you can use to change the world."

Nelson Mandela
Leader of the Anti-Apartheid Movement &
Former President of South Africa

The educational campaigns to build awareness about sexuality launched by Dr. Mahinder C. Watsa in the 1970s continued to grow and expand in later decades. In fact, they became something of a hallmark of the activities of the Family Planning Association of India (FPAI), lifting its work above being merely about contraceptive methods or planning families. The number of workshops, seminars, and conferences were legion; and, as remarked earlier, were widespread – held in India as well as in neighbouring countries. Yet, they were only one of the invaluable initiatives introduced by him.

What was remarkable about Dr. Watsa was that he understood the need for sexuality education in a holistic manner. Yes, he was most concerned that knowledge and information should reach adolescents. But, he also realised the significance of dissemination of information to several other categories. Two amongst these were people whose sheer existence, or professional life, was connected to adolescents, young adults, or young couples and through them to issues of sexuality. These were parents of adolescents and medical professionals. For, without the understanding and support of parents and care givers, young people would find it difficult to cope with their issues. Also, in most cases, general practitioners (GPs) or Family Doctors are the first recourse (if at all!) for troubled parents and youngsters to discuss issues of a sexual nature bothering them; and to seek help to sort themselves out.

At one level, the work with doctors following different systems of medicine as referred to by Dr. Ruby Baam (herself a homeopath) in the last chapter, was what was directly related to the FPAI activities. Here, it was a fairly straightforward discourse on contraception, what was most ideally suited; and how to counsel a couple to use these methods (to medical students, medical professionals, pharmacists and doctors of alternative medicine); and in some instances counselling them on issues of sexuality; and then there were lectures and practical demonstrations on how to do vasectomies and tubectomies (for those doctors who were qualified to do so).

Yet, the country had thousands of doctors in various cities and towns and, of course, even in the rural areas. It was Dr. Mahinder Watsa's ardent wish to spread the good word – scientific information on sexology and sexual and reproductive health – to as many doctors as possible; and as far and wide as feasible; as most of them had very little knowledge about sexuality.

"Some of them were not even willing to admit they did not know," remarks Dr. Reddy. "And Dr. Watsa felt that if the general practitioners were given the knowledge, at least they would cause no further damage to the patient."

It was in 1976 that Dr. Mahinder C. Watsa had struck upon the concept of distance education. He had set up a body called Medikon, and under a subsidiary/division called Medikon Sexual Sciences, he launched a unique distance learning programme, with himself as the Course Director and Dr. Barry McCarthy, PhD, Professor of Psychology & Sex Therapist, as Course Advisor.

Described as a "Correspondence Course on Sex Therapy and Counselling", the programme comprised eight modules. These were, apparently, typed and 'reproduced' – cyclostyled in the early days in all probability – and sent by post to doctors who had enrolled, for a very nominal fee, only enough to cover costs perhaps.

As we know, in the late 1970s, there was no internet – which was eventually made available to the general public starting only on August 15, 1995; and became more popular and widespread only after the start of the new millennium.

Each module of anywhere between 80-100 pages of A4 size paper began with a "Dear Doctor" letter written and signed by Dr. Watsa 'speaking' directly to the physicians, on a topic of relevance to the particular module. It could be detailing out the content, or why a particular theme was being focussed upon or even urging them to study the document and send feedback.

"The interesting thing was that Dr. Watsa would send out one module at a time to the subscribers," recalls Dr. Malde. "When a person had mastered one module, only then did he send the next."

He points out that those days there were hardly any sources for clinical training. "These modules were empowering many doctors," he emphasises. Those who benefitted from the courses included practitioners of general medicine, surgery, virology, dermatology, gynaecology, psychiatry, and pharmacology. Dr. Watsa imparted to them all the basic information on sexuality – the medical side as well as about counselling and psychotherapy.

The measure of how useful, and therefore popular, were these courses can be gauged by the fact that there continued to be a demand for them almost till the end of Dr. Watsa's own life. Of course, by then, the internet had not only been launched but was firmly rooted in the country. Medikon Medical Sciences went up as a website several years back and no doubt helped to spread the word even further. Yet, one thing remained constant – the modules were still sent as before, by post and one at a time!

The "booklets" or the set of course modules seem to have remained much the same over the decades and would not have won any design or printing awards then; and certainly not now, in this age of flash and shine. But what is remarkable is the content – both in terms of the breadth and depth of its coverage. The modules include contributions from some the leading practitioners of sexuality medicine from across the world; carried reprints of articles and essays from prominent sources, as well as material written by Dr. Watsa and some of his colleagues or even simply doctors whose lives he had touched in some way.

The modules covered everything from information about the basics – such as the female and male sex organs, a glossary of sexual terms, phases of life – to the importance of cleanliness; health and its impact on sex life; adolescent fears and conundrums to adult to senior sexual life and the issues confronting people at each stage. It contained detailed instructions on how to question the patients and gather relevant information; how to form a diagnosis; how to help patients improve their interpersonal relations as well as their sex life; and so it went on. Even listing all the aspects covered would take several pages, so comprehensive were the topics expounded upon and the information set forth.

Dr. Watsa had always been very strict in his approach to his work, making sure that all was just so in the manner in which he, his colleagues, and those he trained conducted themselves. This is amply clear in his very first letter to Doctors in Module I (reprinted at the end of this chapter) in which he listed out all the dos and don'ts of a practice as a sexology counsellor and therapist, including the need to maintain ethics at the forefront at all times.

Interestingly, Dr. Watsa's joining FPAI – which don't forget had the advantage of being under the umbrella of an active international body, the IPPF, with its galaxy of experienced experts in the field of sexual reproductive health – greatly facilitated and strengthened the achievement of his goals. With his own dedication, commitment and, most important of all, a vast amount of clinical experience, he was able to quickly make friends and forge strong working bonds with people across the world engaged in the field of sexology.

Even today, his colleagues remember his remarkable connection with the international community whether from the East in Thailand, neighbouring countries like Sri Lanka or then the Western nations like UK and USA amongst others. "He was always able to get the best of the foreign experts when he organised seminars and conferences," recalls Dr. Brahmbhatt.

Perhaps the most eminent amongst all his connections – and certainly of great significance for our tale – was Patricia Schiller, someone with whom Dr. Watsa was to work closely and launch some important initiatives.

Schiller was an American "lawyer, teacher, sexuality educator, sex therapist, and founder and the first ED of the American Association of Sexuality Educators, Counselors, and Therapists (AASECT)".

A liberal thinker and progressive in her outlook, Schiller had done some laudatory work for young women in her country. As an attorney, she learnt, through the divorce cases she handled, that sexual issues between couples were at least a part of the problem which led them to such a point. Like Dr. Watsa and Dr. Soonawala had expressed, such marriages could perhaps have been saved with proper counselling. As a result, Schiller was keen to take up counselling, but she needed formal training for this.

While pursuing a degree in clinical psychology, Schiller had taken up a teaching job. At the college she was horrified to learn that pregnant teenagers were often abandoned by the boys/men who had got them pregnant; and also faced the opprobrium of society, maybe even of their own parents; and were often "condemned to a life of poverty".

"By founding a school in Washington DC to educate pregnant schoolgirls, Schiller helped to shatter American taboos on teenage sex long before the birth of the Swinging Sixties," AASECT says.

On another note, what is interesting is the reaction accorded to her in the America of those early days. "Her work as a sex counsellor often elicited amusement, tinged with embarrassment, among friends," one report said.

"They say, 'Ha ha, there's the dirty old lady, there's the sex maniac,' but I don't mind. I enjoy it," Schiller told *The Washington Post* in 1978.

Reactions which very much mirror the situation in India described earlier.

It was in 1967 that she had set up AASECT, as a body that would eventually train and certify sexuality educators and clinicians – several thousands of them in fact. She herself had switched careers earlier and moved from being a Legal Aid Society attorney to becoming a sexuality educator, first at school and then at a medical college. "Ms. Schiller initiated AASECT's certification program in 1972, with the help of top sexual health professionals, including Albert Ellis, William Masters, and Virginia Johnson."

In an aside, for those who have not been intimately connected with the field of sexology, Masters and Johnson were, and still are, considered the ultimate on Sexuality Studies.

They conducted a lot of research on the subject and are considered the pioneers whose work advanced the "scientific study of human sexuality". In 1964 they set up the Reproductive Biology Research Foundation, which was later renamed the Masters & Johnson Institute. At the peak of its operations (the Institute shut down in 1994), the Institute was a bubbling cauldron of multi-disciplinary medical personnel involved in a fairly new field of work. It also ran a programme to train sex therapists, organised seminars and workshops at different places. Apart from all this, "the institute also spearheaded a drive during the 1970s to establish ethical guidelines for sex educators, therapists, and researchers".

Patricia Schiller, in the meantime, had also felt a great need for some certifying agency so that both standards and ethics of the profession could be protected. Hence AASECT.

"Professionalising the fields of sex education, counselling, and therapy, then taking AASECT international, were among Schiller's lasting legacies," says William Stayton, a professor emeritus and former director of the Center for Human Sexuality Studies at Widener University in Chester, PA, USA, as quoted by *The Lancet* in an obituary which appeared in the online version on August 18, 2018.

In India, working in the ob-gyn field, Dr. Watsa had also developed a similar outlook – the imperative need for sex education, the need to spread the word as far and wide as possible; as well as to ensure that the practice of sexuality education, counselling and therapy should be conducted with the highest standards of ethical probity and the practitioners should also be above reproach in their conduct.

When the two met up in the 1970s, it was only natural that they should have found much in common. In many ways, both shared an almost identical missionary zeal on the subject. As mentioned above, both had perceived the need to widen the sphere of their influence and bring in newer sections within their purview, so to say.

Much enthused with her ideas, which dovetailed with his own, and the concept of an organisation she had set up, Dr. Watsa proposed the setting up of a similar one in India.

Receiving enthusiastic backing from Avabai Wadia, he along with Patricia Schiller founded the Council of Sex Education and Parenthood (International) (abbreviated to CSEP(I) or CSEPI). Though it had started off with a slightly different name, CSEPI is what it has been most popularly known as for many decades now.

He also took on the role as Editor of the quarterly "ICSEP News & Views" which was supplied free to the members regularly.

"Dr. Watsa as a convener arranged a meeting of seven senior consultants – Dr. R.H. Dastur, Dr. C. L. Jhaveri, Mrs. Sarla Mukhi, Dr. Esther Dubey, Dr. Vithal Prabhu, Dr. Raj Brahmbhatt, where it was decided to form the International Council of Sex Education and Parenthood – ICSEP [later known as Council of Sex Education and Parenthood (International)], which with the wise advice of Dr. Patricia agreed to affiliate the Council to the International Council of Sex Education and Parenthood in Washington D.C. which was headed by her and had members from all parts of the world. Currently CSEPI is affiliated to the World Association for Sexual Health," outlines the website of CSEPI.

"Dr. Watsa believed that even parents can be educators," elaborates Dr. Brahmbhatt. "You can be a natural or a trained counsellor. Where counselling is concerned, there are skills involved – where an untrained person may take two days to grasp the problem; for a skilled, trained counsellor it would take only four questions to get to the root of the matter – then would come the aspect of therapy."

In March of 1982, the Council was founded and registered at the Public Trusts Registration Office. Soon after, in the same year, the organisation held its first National Conference in Mumbai. Ever since then, the annual conference has become a regular feature – in the tradition set by Dr. Watsa himself.

"Thanks to the support of Avabai Wadia, we were allocated Rs. 22 lakh for CSEPI," remembers Dr. Brahmbhatt, the organisation's sole surviving founder today. "Dr. Watsa was Avabai Wadia's blue-eyed boy – because he was a visionary, she gave him full support."

Even later, private contributions, including from Ms. Wadia's trust helped to keep CSEPI well funded.

The organisation's Mission and Vision Statements encapsulate Dr. Watsa's own beliefs in a nutshell. While it outlined its Mission as "... the development and advancement of the field of Sexual Health (Sex Education, Sex Counseling, Sex Therapy and Sexual Medicine)," it also stressed (in keeping with Dr. Watsa's emphasis on ethics): "CSEPI's mission is the advancement of the highest standards of professional practice for educators, counselors, therapists and Sexual Health Physicians."

In its 'Vision of Sexual Health', the organisation iterates: "CSEPI affirms the fundamental value of sexuality as an inherent, essential, and beneficial dimension of being human."

Though it is a statement ahead of its times, it does not stop there. Carrying on in a stronger voice, it goes on to say: "In general, CSEPI opposes all psychological, social, cultural, legislative and governmental forces that would restrict, curtail or interfere with the fundamental values of sexual health and sexual freedom that we espouse. CSEPI also opposes all abuses of sexuality including, but not limited to, harassment, intimidation, coercion, prejudice, and the infringement of any individual's sexual and civil rights."

It is worth putting down here excerpts from the Value Statements affirmed by CSEPI, which form part of the Mission and Vision section of its website. Together with the Mission and Vision of Sexual Health Statements, the Value Statements serve to heavily underscore and put the spotlight on the liberal, tolerant, inclusive, and open-minded outlook which Dr. Watsa not only believed in and upheld, but actively fostered amongst all those he came in contact with.

(Excerpted but otherwise reproduced as it appears)

CSEPI affirms the following VALUE STATEMENTS:

Sexual Health: *CSEPI believes in promoting Sexual Health, when it is ethical, consensual and non-risky (both physical and emotional).*

Sexual Health Education: *There is an urgent need for comprehensive education about Sexual Health to be made available to all people. CSEPI advocates for social, cultural, political, and economic changes to expand, and extend the availability of quality education in Sexual Health. CSEPI believes that Scientific and Accessible education for sexual health must respect the beliefs as well as the cultural and individual practices of the people.*

Adolescent Sexual Health: *CSEPI advocates for the Sexual Health and Rights of adolescents, for their protection as well as for their education, and CSEPI therefore opposes all forces that would restrict or interfere with the entitlement of adolescents to develop in a sexually healthy manner that is age-appropriate, and entirely free from adult exploration.*

Sexual Equality: *CSEPI recognizes that sexuality is multi dimensional and encompasses all forms of Sexuality: Sexual Orientations, Gender, Transgender and Intersex as erotic preferences and lifestyles. They should be considered non judgmentally. CSEPI opposes the use of labels such as normal and abnormal to these variations in the healthy sexual expression of adults. CSEPI believes that all sexual and cultural minorities should enjoy sexual freedom, equal civil rights, and parity of social opportunities and privileges.*

Sexual Health Rights: *CSEPI believes that every individual has a right to Sexual Health. For this all individuals should be supported in seeking and finding opportunities to pursue a healthy and happy sexual life of their own choosing.*

CSEPI recognizes that the right to pursue a healthy and happy sexual life applies to all individuals, especially those with special needs or challenges, as well as with significant medical conditions.

CSEPI recognizes and supports the right of all individuals to have access to the best available technologies for reproductive decision-making, and to individually-governed freedom of choice of all matters pertaining to Reproduction and Family Planning.

Sexual Health Care: *CSEPI recognizes the prevalence of sexual practices that are unhealthy, and unhappy and acknowledges that many people struggle with sexual distress, disorder and dysfunction. CSEPI believes that there is an urgent need for therapeutic intervention and for personal growth opportunities to be made available to all people, who are compromised in their pursuit of sexual health and happiness provided in a manner that secures the client's or patient's privacy, confidentiality and self-respect. CSEPI will remain vigilant about and support those issues pertaining to sexual health and sexual rights wherever and whenever the opinion of the professional expertise that we represent might exert a positive influence.*

"Soon after the organisation became functional, we launched a publication called *Flash* to be able to disseminate information widely on its behalf," remembers Dr. Brahmbhatt, who has now been designated as the Founder Trustee & Editor Emeritus of CSEPI. "We used to organise several all-India conferences in those days, for which Dr. Watsa and I travelled together a lot; within India as well as to neighbouring countries like Sri Lanka."

In the course of organising the various public conferences, as well as participating in international ones, Dr. Watsa would interact with a number of international experts: at the core there was Dr. Patricia Schiller founder-director of AASECT; and Peter and Gill Gordon, sponsored by IPPF. It was these stalwarts who, along with a few other international like-minded doctors also became the mainstay resource for the various conferences and educational activities organised by Dr. Watsa in India and abroad. Some of these like-minded individuals included Shirley Zussman, John Money, Barry McCarthy, Janet Wolfe, June Reinisch, Leonard Rosenblum, Leonore Tiefer, Brunhild Kring, Hani Miletski, Mark Schwartz, Susan Lee (all from USA); John Bancroft, Douglas Hooper, Richard Green (UK); Milton Diamond (Hawaii); Alessandra Graziottini (Italy); L.J.G. Gooren (Netherlands); Emil Ng (Hong Kong); Ganesan Adaikan (Singapore); Nikorn Dusitsin, Palarp Sinhaseni (Thailand); Jane Keany, Margaret Redelman (Australia).

Dr. Watsa also developed links with other organisations like the Indian Council of Medical Research (ICMR); National Institute for Research in Reproductive & Child Health (NIRRCH); Centre for Organisational Research & Training (CORT), Vadodara; Tata Institute of Social Sciences (TISS), Mumbai.

Another pioneering step taken by him – which actually flows from the points in the Value Statements of CSEPI – was his work with what was then known as The Spastics Society of India; today, it has refashioned itself as ADAPT (Able Disabled All People Together). It was set up as an NGO to help people with neuro-muscular and developmental disabilities. While there was thought put into educating youngsters suffering from these problems, no one had even considered that they also have sexual needs and frustrations. It was to Dr. Watsa's credit that he not only perceived that they may be facing problems, but was also able to reach out and communicate with, and counsel them.

"He was the first person who teamed up with the Spastics Society and brought out a manual for them," affirms Dr. Reddy. "In that he was a pioneer of working with young people with special needs."

Incidentally, a critically acclaimed film, *Margarita with a Straw*, starring Kalki Koechlin, was based on just such a theme – the coming of age of a person with disabilities. The production, which won several awards including for the film, for the director, Shonali Bose, as well as for lead actor Kalki, is perhaps the only such Indian work made on this theme.

The late 1980s and the 1990s were a period when the HIV-AIDS epidemic took quite a grip on the Indian population, with the first cases being detected in 1986. While the early victims were sex workers, and those from the Men-who-have-Sex-with-Men (MSM) segment, soon monogamous housewives too were getting infected by their husbands who were clearly playing the field. This immediately opened up the possibility of children being infected as well.

Towards the end of the 1980s, AIDS was a very serious concern and the authorities nationally were mobilising resources to tackle the epidemic through education, for prevention and management.

Needless to say, Dr. Watsa also organised his own brigade to lead the charge against the dreaded disease.

"We had created four modules on AIDS awareness as sexual education was considered very important," recalls Dr. Brahmbhatt. "Again, we had the support of international experts – there were Peter and Gill Gordon working with us on the on HIV-AIDS issue."

In fact, the support of the vast network that Dr. Watsa had created proved invaluable at this time. Also, the initiative to involve doctors of the Indian Systems of Medicine in reproductive health to work in an

"Action Now" programme resulted in the involvement of more than 15,000 doctors in Mumbai.

By now, Dr. Watsa had not only trained thousands of doctors to undertake sexuality medicine, but he had also trained several hundreds of sociologists and psychologists to be able to educate and counsel those in need of it. This brigade has been doing a stellar, if uphill job since then.

Towards the end of the 1990s, came a development which was to be something of a game changer for the world – well at least for men with erectile dysfunction, which is one of the most widespread sexuality issues faced by men.

The drug Sildenafil, which was being developed since 1989 as a medication for hypertension and angina pectoris by Pfizer researchers, was found to have unexpected side-effects – it was able to "cure" erectile dysfunction and allow men with the issue to perform. After due process, it was introduced as Viagra in the UK and US in 1998; and reached the Indian market in December 2005. But already, by 2001, various local alternatives had been developed by Indian pharmaceutical companies and were available in the country.

"When Viagra was introduced in 1998, the publicity it got really woke up the medical profession from slumber," says Dr. Narayana Reddy.

ARMING MEDICS WITH KNOWLEDGE

Medikon Sexual Sciences proved to be a most effective platform for reaching out to doctors in various parts of the country. Over a period of a few decades, innumerable doctors were able to arm themselves with the knowledge and skills required to address issues of sexual health, whatever be their original persuasion. In the process, Dr. Watsa was able to provide yet another salutary service, which would have a beneficial impact on vast communities of people.

Reproduced below is the letter addressed to doctors participating in the programme in the first Module of papers.

Medikon Sexual Sciences
Correspondence Course on
Sex Therapy and Counselling

Introductory Letter in Module - I

Dear Doctor,
Please read this before starting your training programmes. Sigmund Freud, the famous psychoanalyst, was attempting to understand an exceedingly puzzling set of symptoms in a hysterical woman who had responded to none of his attempts at treatment. An older colleague who knew the circumstances of the case remarked that this patient would certainly be cured if only the physician could write the prescription, "A normal penis repeated several times".

Freud describes the revelation that this statement was for him as he first realised that sexual needs when frustrated and denied can induce symptoms. He bitterly reflected that if such factors were involved in the genesis of human suffering, they were never taught to him in a school of medicine and no mention was ever made of them.

We are in the same position in India today. This training programme will help to correct this void in your knowledge. It will touch upon some basics that are necessary to understand and treat sexual concerns and dysfunctions in your clinic.

Naturally, all matters in human sexuality cannot and will not be covered. Should you wish for more details over and above what we shall send you, please write and we shall try and help you.

Please note:

Each mailing will have a code on the top right hand corner, for example, M-I indicates that it is the first mailing of the course. M-II indicates that it is the second mailing.

Each mailing will have several reprints, articles, etc., in it. The second number indicates the order in which the articles have to be studied by you, For e.g. M-I-1, M-I-2

We would strongly advise you to keep all the material in a serial order for quick and easy reference.

For quicker understanding we shall try to keep the language we use as simple as possible. After reading please try and draw out questions for which the answers are in the text. Please also try and note what is important and relevant to be utilised in your practice - of course, we shall help you, a good way is to recollect a case you have come across and analyse how you would solve it.

Knowledge may be acquired through reading; skills through putting the knowledge in practice, but in addition to the usual skills required, you must become comfortable, with your own

sexuality. After all, how can you tell a person that it is all right to masturbate if you do not believe it yourself?

1. How much knowledge do you have? You need not feel anxious when you answer true/false on the sheet supplied. These tests are only to stimulate curiosity and draw your attention to some of the issues.
2. Personal ethics in dealing with sexual problems must always be at the forefront of your behaviour. Please read note on The Physician and Ethics.
3. We need to lower the veil that we all put on when we are confronted by sensitive issues. We shall attempt to desensitise so that you can face any client without feeling embarrassed, tense or resentful. In sexual matters what do you feel? Excited? Tense? Anxious? Can you objectively see the problem and counsel?

In M-I we are enclosing some explicit pictures. Please look at them, write down your frank thoughts and feelings - unless you are honest with yourself you will never make a satisfactory sex therapist and counsellor.

We shall value your comments, criticisms, praises and any suggestions to improve this programme. We wish you many hours of pleasure studying with us.

Yours sincerely,
Dr. Mahinder C. Watsa

CHAPTER 8

PENMANSHIP TO THE FORE

2000s-2010s

The new millennium dawned with much excitement and anticipation.

One of its more significant features has been the rise of the Internet, which saw a phase of rapid development over both the decades. In the 2000s, there were many social networking sites which made an appearance, culminating with the emergence of Facebook as the leader in 2009.

In India, the population crossed the one billion mark in May 2000.

The brutal rape of a woman in New Delhi, in 2012, which galvanised the conscience of the nation, showed that even in the 21st century women were still not safe. The continuing, barbaric incidents, which victimised young girls and women alike, in later years too, further underscored this.

The big development worldwide was the emergence of social media which has become both a medium to mobilise public opinion and people around just causes; as well as a platform through which to troll, harass and hound people.

Perhaps the most noteworthy aspect of the 2010s, one for which it will go down in historic memory, is the new virus which emerged at the end of that decade, as if from a Pandora's Box; and rapidly circumnavigated the globe, doing a veritable death dance along the way.

"You are never too old to set another goal or to dream a new dream."

C. S. Lewis
Writer

As the curtain goes up on the decade of the new millennium, we find Dr. Watsa concentrating more on his private consulting practice for sexuality counselling and therapy work.

By now, the clinic in the cottage on Hill Road, in Mumbai's happening suburb Bandra, had been redeveloped and he had set up a Polyclinic in the space allocated to him. The cottage clinic is still remembered in many, many houses in Bandra where the now grown-up men – who were treated by him as children – live with their own families.

Dr. Watsa's own practice had shifted entirely to Sunder House, where a lift was eventually fitted in to enable him to go up and down without straining himself. For, in the year 2001, when this shift took place, he was just three years short of his 80th birthday.

He had bid an official farewell to FPAI in 1995, until which time he was committed to the organisation on a full time basis. However, Dr. Watsa was soon back working with the organisation in a consulting position as a volunteer, and continued his outreach programmes and other campaigns in a vigorous manner.

In fact, in the year 2002, he was named the Vice President of the national body, and President of the Mumbai Branch. He was also President of the FPAI from 2003 to 2008. These were positions very important to him, as he was invested in the FPAI, body, heart, mind and soul.

At the same time, he was also designated as Founder Chairman of CSEPI – which he had been since its inception. Today, he remains on its marquee as the Founder; and though he was apparently named as President Emeritus somewhere along the way, that position seems to have lapsed with his passing.

Far from slowing down, or even retiring, on his 81st birthday, Dr. Watsa was actually poised to strike out in a … well one can't say entirely new pursuit, for he had done something similar all his life. But yes, on a new platform – and certainly with entirely unexpected consequences. The outcome of one small decision – a simple yes – was to catapult him to the Social Hall of Fame; and take him, as well as all around him by storm. Though him, admittedly, least of all. Because in his typical calm, understated manner, though he expressed pleasure in the response, he showed no signs that he was particularly flattered by it; in fact, his colleagues had often remarked how modest he was, and how he never had any sense of ego.

What was this momentous development which hinged on a simple "Yes"? Well as you might have guessed after connecting the dots – it was the launch of his column *Ask the Sexpert* in *Mumbai Mirror*.

With its launch, there was an avalanche of mail for Dr. Watsa, and his popularity only increased with each sparkling and piquant reply. Soon he came to be known as "The Sexpert"; and his fans, like a benevolent tsunami, lifted him and his reputation up and up and carried him ever higher and ever forward on their shoulders. That much was evident from the opening pages of this book. But what had wrought this huge difference now, given that Dr. Watsa had been counselling people and doling out advice for over four decades prior to this? Was it mere chance? Was it that he was saying something different? Or was it that he had found a better medium through which to put forward his thoughts?

His enhanced and pronounced popularity and stupendous success was the result of a coalescing of several factors, and all of the above.

One important aspect, of course, was the sheer passage of time and developments over the period which had led to some change in the demographics and social ethos of the moment. Within a section of elite society, the adolescents and young adults of 1973 – when he started out on his career as a sexologist – were themselves adults now with teenage or slightly older children of their own. These parents had two things going for them – they grew up in a fairly liberal world themselves (if not at home, in the general environment); and travel, internet, and exposure through various media had caused a cross fertilisation of thoughts and ideas. To whatever extent, they raised their children with a slightly more open attitude. So, their children already had a lot of exposure to sexology, even if it wasn't through channelised scientific education.

At another level, there had been a great burgeoning of the middle class especially as a result of the economic spurt in development in the 1990s and early years of the new millennium, when India's development – measured by GDP growth – soon outpaced many of the large western powers and the country was poised to make a leap in its advancement. While many of these families may have a fairly traditional and conservative ethos at home, they too were exposed to modern media and hence were more open in their minds. An entire generation of adolescents accepted their sexuality, even if it was in private or within a small group of same-sex friends. They realised that they had questions – but even if they did not necessarily admit it in polite society or in their homes, they felt, by and large, it was okay to be inquisitive about their bodies, and to entertain these questions in their minds.

That was where society as a whole was poised, when the column was first launched in March 2005. The *Mumbai Mirror,* the vehicle for the column, was the home product of Bennett, Coleman & Co. Ltd., publishers of *The Times of India*, the country's largest circulating daily newspaper. Moreover, not only was it the largest, it was headed by a very marketing savvy management. Thus, *Mumbai Mirror* got an editorial profile, the get up and the push to make it very popular with a young readership.

What the paper also had going for it was an editor with a keen sense of what would work with a publication's target viewership group. Recognising that sexual concerns were fairly high on the list of matters of interest to its readership, she went out of her way to identify the correct person to do a column on these matters.

Without *Mumbai Mirror's* editor being quite aware of it, Dr. Mahinder C. Watsa had by this time been "conversing" with adolescents and young adults – and also older persons – for well over 40 years, maybe almost 45 years. For, his journey as a columnist had begun in the late 1950s. And it had picked up momentum since his joining of FPAI in 1973, through booklets and meetings and workshops. There was little that troubled the minds of youngsters that he was not aware of or knew about. Years of interaction, perhaps enhanced by the *Mumbai Mirror* approach and his own advancing years combined with his natural wit, did add an acerbic twist to his answers. Always direct and not at all one to mince his words, Dr. Watsa added humour to the mix to evolve a very particular brand of an Agony Aunt column that no one else could write or even imitate – that would take even a clever person time and practise to evolve.

The youngsters loved it! There was no beating about the bush or dancing around the trees. Dr. Watsa's piercing answers were shot as straight and true as Cupid's own arrow!

An entire section of young people was buying the *Mirror* only to read The Sexpert. The writings would be avidly devoured either singly or in small groups, over many "Oohs" and "Aahs".

Perhaps what also gave a great fillip to Dr. Watsa's and the column's popularity was the development of modern social media. In a year down the line from its launch, Twitter came on the scene and after another few years, there was WhatsApp, and India saw the widespread use of Smartphones.

Digital media had another peculiarity – it allowed, and even encouraged, users to be "aggregative". One cell (phone) naturally tended to gravitate to another, so to speak! And, it was not just conversations or messaging between people on a one-to-one basis. Rather, there was a tendency to aggregate, much like fat cells, or any other cell-based structure. And so, we soon had WhatsApp groups – when the phenomenon was introduced – around 'Watsaisms', twitter broadcasting lists prepared by the fans of the best of Dr. Watsa and so on. Riding along on this wave of popularity as he was, it was only natural that the opportunity to encompass all his learnings and teachings – yes, the latter emanated from the former, so the two were intrinsically, inextricably intertwined – in one compendium, sooner or later presented itself. It was a long cherished goal of his to write a book and it so came to pass that renowned publishers Penguin Books and celebrated sexologist, The Sexpert, came together to disseminate his wisdom. The result? His book, *'It's Normal!'* published in March 2015.

Dr. Mahinder C. Watsa had just turned 91 years old. It is difficult to recall anyone who accomplished a similar feat. And mind you, it was not an "As Told To" or a ghost-written piece of work. It was a book that he himself, personally – to stress and stretch the point! – had laboured over. Collecting, compiling, collating his writings, his Q/As. Creating a skeleton structure for the book, writing fresh bits to flesh it out and link the various bits with muscle and tendons.

"Experience has taught me not to be surprised by surprises," Dr. Watsa wrote in the Preface to the book. "Over forty-five years of practice, and answering 40,000 plus questions from people who have sexual concerns often as a result of lack of knowledge or misconceptions, have resulted in this book."

Disclaiming that it is no "treatise on sexuality", he assured readers that everyone would find something in it to enhance their knowledge or solve their sexual problems.

"It might help save one from the trap of a quack who sells untested, advertised treatment which could cause harm or have other adverse effects," he said referring to another bugbear of all genuine, scientific sexologists – phony practitioners.

Over his decades of practice, Dr. Watsa said, he had often been asked by people: "Am I normal?" This question was raised sometimes with a genuinely troubled mind, in relation to the problems they were confiding to the sexologist, and sometimes "seeking permission for their actions".

To all the queries which were put to him, he answered each one in a reassuring manner, and these indicate just how open minded he was. Very little fazed him; even less disconcerted him. As far as sexual desires and practices went, he was very tolerant of the different strokes represented by the wide canvas of humanity he had encountered.

However, there was one fundamental principle he held very dear, and insisted that everyone follow: all sexual interaction **must** be **consensual** and must in **no way** cause physical or mental harm to the partner. This included his major taboos – incest, violence and force. All else was par for the course. As long as it was enjoyable to both partners and caused no harm to either of them or anyone else.

The only other aspect which he found objectionable – and therefore which gave rise to his caustic comments – was unscientific foolishness, which he just didn't seem to be able to tolerate. His columns and various Q/A compilations are scattered with many delectable exchanges that such interactions have given rise to!

Like everything else he did, the book is a very thorough compilation covering not only a range of issues but, importantly, addressing concerns affecting people across age segments and demographic groups.

At one level it speaks to the adolescent or young adult, providing thorough, scientific knowledge about male and female bodies and sex organs. And if any layperson thought they knew it all, they have a thought coming. Just to give one example, in the course of describing the female sex organs, he says that the vagina, "The passageway for the birth of a baby, and the discharge of the menstrual fluid from the uterus is not a single tube. The 'vagina' is a series of elastic rings put together.

This allows the different sizes of the penis to comfortably fit into it." And in a few sentences, Dr. Watsa has probably put to rest a large percentage of queries and anxieties. For, the predominant apprehension among men is about size and performance. The scientific approach would indicate that there is no physical reason that sexual relations between two persons should not be fulfilling and satisfactory whatever the size of the sexual organ, in most cases.

At other levels the book also addresses questions confronting adults and seniors; and issues confronting both men and women.

There are myriad gems encrusted throughout the book, if one is inclined to look for them. For some, it might be an exercise akin to stepping into a minefield. For, no doubt there are several people who still have many inhibitions and find it difficult to face up to, or even consider, talking about the subject; thus, they may find the explicit nature of the book a trifle difficult to negotiate. Yet, as Dr. Watsa said, there is something, some bit of wisdom there for everyone.

To sample a few choice ones, some excerpts:

(Addressing Teens and Youth)

"All human beings are sexual... Learning about sexuality begins when a child is born and continues until the end of life.

"Going through life is a wonderful journey full of excitement and surprises. The early years of life are, up to twenty years of age, characterised by physical growth, emotional changes and rich experience. Sexuality affects all three, that is, growth, emotional change and experience."

Just the tone of his words puts sex and sexuality on an extremely even plane and something to be accepted and embraced. Their timbre is certainly not of the sanctimonious or slightly squeamish manner in which knowledge on the subject is generally imparted.

Then there is this (as printed in the book)

THERE'S A DIFFERENCE BETWEEN SEXUAL DESIRE AND LOVE

Sexual desire is strong physical excitement. Love is a powerful feeling of caring for someone else.

Sex needs caring and sharing, it involves responsibility and an equal partnership.

Sex partners need to share responsibility for birth control. They should also protect each other from infections.

Remember this was something which Dr. Watsa had been emphasising one way or the other since he first began practising as a sexologist and even earlier when he practised as a Family Physician.

Then there is this gentle, open-hearted, inclusive embracing of all kinds and shades of sexuality as evident in his words below.

DIFFERENT KINDS OF SEXUAL ATTRACTION

Some men are attracted to women, some are not. They may be interested in relationships with other men, or with both women and men. No one knows for sure what makes men gay, bisexual or heterosexual. Sexual orientation develops naturally – perhaps even before birth.

Our society doesn't always help men and women understand the real feelings about sex. It's okay to ignore the pressure to be sexually active; the individual should just be true to himself/herself.

What is of relevance to all, and contains the quintessence of his philosophy, are the four Ts. Again and again, and in different ways, Dr. Watsa stressed them as the foundation of all healthy sexual relationships.

"The 4 Ts are important for mutual happiness," he writes in *It's Normal!* "TRUST in each other cannot be less than 100 per cent; TIME to spend with each other is often neglected; TOUCH, understanding, caring for each other's sexual needs; and most important, TALKING with each other to sort out problems and clear misunderstandings can bring lifelong happiness."

It's Normal! truly addresses questions confronting every group of persons and on a variety of issues.

The core essence of the book is the Q/A section which could be said to be Dr. Watsa's forte and USP in a sense, at least in the earlier days and till fairly recently. Today, there are many who follow the same path; but hardly any can traverse the road in the same inimical style, with the same verve or evoke the same delight amongst readers. The book compiles a vast number of such interactions, probably from different sources (of his own work) and from different periods.

Right till the end, and probably even after, till his fans finally came to terms with his passing, the questions kept pouring in. And they would all get answered – or almost all. For, it was only towards the very end that he stopped replying to them. By then, *Mumbai Mirror,* in its original avatar, had closed down too. In the final years it was that column which more than anything else gave Dr. Watsa a sense of purpose, a push to look forward to each day, as he felt he was helping someone, somewhere deal with problems related to sexuality.

There had been a setback when his beloved wife Promila, passed away in 2006. She had been a pillar of strength standing firmly by his side all throughout his extraordinary life. All his friends and colleagues who were closest to him remember her most fondly and are full of praise for the relationship between the two.

Just how deeply affected he was by her loss can be gauged by the way he responds to questions about her passing in the film which was made on him. Even though he does not say much or anything dramatic, the melancholy is so evident as he talks about her and opens her cupboard and takes out her sarees and lays them on the bed. There is a stark loneliness in knowing that they will never again be worn by the woman he loved. Perhaps they evoked all the warm memories when the sarees had draped her.

And then there was the dedication in *It's Normal!*

"To Promila, my lifelong companion who steadfastly held my hand through the thick and thin of our life. Always giving, never expecting anything but love. I owe her a lot."

A simple enough eulogy; but one that captured a lifetime of togetherness and the solid edifice that was their relationship.

Death may be a capricious brigand and no one knows when he will rob you of that which is most precious; but Life, in her own way, is a cruel taskmaster. For, Life must, and does go on. No one knew that better than Dr. Mahinder C. Watsa. Hadn't he brought innumerable lives into the world? Hadn't he seen Life grow from a seed to a sapling to a tree? And hadn't he shared the most agonising traumas and tribulations of both men and women in the course of them leading their lives?

In the year 2006, at the time of Promila's passing, Dr. Watsa was little over 81 years of age. He had just mounted the roller coaster ride of *Mumbai Mirror* barely a year previously. For, while it was to take him to tremendous heights, it was also a ride with its detractors; a few die-hard conservatives who were opposed to sex education, and entangled him in a sheaf of cases in different courts across the country as Meenal Baghel has outlined earlier.

And so, Life with all that it brought in the way of patients, questions, problems, attending conferences, entanglements with detractors, and meetings with friends covered the wound of his loss with a scab.

We have seen how those years progressed and the name and fame that they brought him. The Earth kept spinning; many years passed. The decade of the 2000s, yielded to the decade of the 2010s.

At some time, when he was almost 90 years old, he was asked about how he felt.

"I do not feel my age," he said (in an interview) with a twinkle in his eye, veritably rubbing his hands in pleasure. "How can I? I have so much to look forward to each day and so much to do, so many people to help."

Virtually till the end, his life was indeed full. There was his work and interaction with colleagues and those who worked with him. There was his family – now including, apart from his son and daughter-in-law, two granddaughters, a grandson-in law and great grandson as well – and there were his friends.

Then came the lockdown. Life was turned on its head and virtually all interaction with the outside world came to a halt. Just prior to this, Dr. Watsa himself had suffered a brief illness which had necessitated hospitalisation. In fact, his 95th birthday, which fell on February 11, 2019, was celebrated from his hospital bed. Even then, he had been quite cheerful and ready to get back to life as usual. But the illness had left him weakened and the enforced isolation as a result of the lockdown from early 2020 didn't help.

On December 28, 2020 Dr. Mahinder C. Watsa departed from this world, leaving the future of his mission in the hands of the doughty army of thousands of scientifically trained professionals he had mentored, guided and imbued with his vision.

The world was never going to be the same after 2020, for more reasons than one. It would no longer have a Dr. Mahinder C. Watsa, the standard bearer and defender of all things that worked to create a sexually inclusive, knowledgeable world, where all people would know their rights and youngsters would be able to defend themselves.

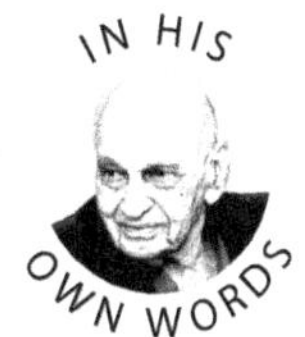

FOREARMED WITH KNOWLEDGE

In the eighth and final module of the Medikon Sexual Sciences course material for doctors of various persuasions, is included a piece (reproduced below) on how to prepare couples for their married life. It has several pertinent pointers.

The module ends with a comprehensive Evaluation Questionnaire for the doctors; and, importantly, a feedback form for the organisers and a final sign-off letter (also reproduced below) from Dr. Watsa, which is quite revealing on the uniqueness of such a course.

Pre-Marital Counselling

Dr. M.C. Watsa

The concept of Pre-marital Counselling is not really there in the Indian context. This could be attributed to the following facts:

a) The younger people believe that things happen naturally.
b) Older experienced people are too embarrassed to give advice.
c) Ignorance breeds ignorance and this has been passed down from generation to generation as far as sex is concerned. In fact the greatest single factor responsible for sexual problems and marital conflicts is ignorance.
d) Young people do not get enough opportunities to discuss with their parents their future before marriage.
e) Although the larger metropolitan cities have seen the mushrooming of counselling centres, these services are still not sufficient to cater to the young people, nor do they feel any urge to utilise the services.

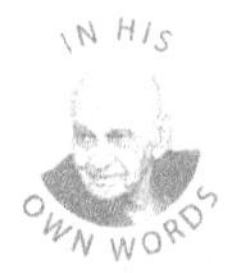

It is important that counselling pre-marital couples must involve both partners, often only the male turns up. In our Centre, pre-marital counselling takes into consideration the following facts:

Attitudes:

Counselling is started on a low key as attitudes, customs and traditions are long standing. Both should have the correct attitude towards marriage and this is the counsellor's important task. They should have an understanding of what goes to make a successful marriage. There is no success formula. A successful marriage is largely a question of adjustment of three kinds: it must include harmony of the mind, body and spirit. They should be told that in the beginning both partners must inevitably feel shy, entertain fears and doubts. Also that 'a trouble shared is a trouble halved' - which brings us to a very important factor, communication. A marriage where there is no communication is heading for the rocks, as all their negative feelings now become hidden grievances and thus sources of silent estrangement.

Aspirations vs Realistic Expectations:

Very often young people enter marriage with a view that from now on it will be only a long glorious honeymoon. They must be made aware of the realities and practicalities, of newer responsibilities which they have to undertake. In our experience many rifts in marriage are due to unmet expectations.

Sexual Advice:

Before entering marriage, they should have a clear idea of their bodies and its functions and how they work in the sex act. Any myths and misconceptions about the size of the penis, the hymen, etc., should be removed. They should be made aware of how both of them react differently to the sex act by virtue of being a male or a female.

Reasons for Sex Act:
Need for procreation and as an outward physical expression of love which is satisfying to both partners. Both points are equally important and should be stressed. Sexual advice should cover aspects of the first night trauma, the sex act, etc. a physical examination of both partners is essential but the female rarely submits to an examination. Tests should be administered to determine the blood group RH factor and for the presence of sexually transmitted disease.

Responsible Parenthood:
To be responsible parents, physical maturity, emotional maturity and the economic capacity to provide and protect the family is required. Planning a family is very important, particularly in today's context. It is necessary to have a smaller but healthier family. Spacing of children is equally important to all concerned. Hence the counsellor will spend a considerable time in explaining and planning with the couple when the first child should be born and what should be a suitable contraceptive for them. We often find ignorance and misconception of the condom and the pill. Family planning and contraceptive advice should also be given.

In conclusion, it can be said that the largest population in India belongs to the age group 15-25 and therefore, it is imperative that they be involved in the family planning programme. Not just the pre-marital group, but the 'just married group as well'.

Evaluation of the Correspondence Course on Sex Therapy and Counselling

Dear Doctor,
We are pleased you have completed this course. No such correspondence course exists in any developing country. In fact, our search in the U.K. and U.S.A. also does not reveal any similar course. In this pioneering effort we solicit your help. We would like your frank comments, criticisms and suggestions. Please feel free to add any observations to those in the attached sheet. We shall appreciate it and thank you for it because it will help us to continually improve the course.

Please conclude by any statement you would like to make including the get-up, presentation, reprints, cassette, the teaching method, the teacher etc.

Thank you for your co-operation.

Yours Sincerely
Sd/-
Mahinder C. Watsa
Course Director

CHAPTER 9

THE *KARMAYOGI*

1950-2020

From youth to old age: such a long journey. A distance traversed by most people. Yet, each passage encompassing a different route, a different destination. Some make history, others become history. A few are remembered by more than their immediate circle. Others leave a lasting impression on the society they lived in, leaving permanent impressions in the shifting sands of time.

"Do not follow where the path may lead. Go instead where there is no path and leave a trail."

Ralph Waldo Emerson
Poet, Essayist & Abolitionist

In the seven decades or so that Dr. Mahinder C. Watsa was active on the work front, he must have interacted professionally and personally with literally thousands and thousands of people – not counting the exchanges with all the letter writers and question raisers for his columns, which itself constituted a mind-boggling number.

It is amazing that amongst all these people there were hardly any – one can even say none – who had a single unkind thing to say about him or fault him in any way; except of course those who were opposed to him on principle: on the basis that they opposed sex education, or the open discussion of sex in any way, especially for/with children. But that's another matter altogether. Rather, praise from his colleagues, juniors and friends was always of the most fulsome kind; and, what is telling, is all of them reiterate similar qualities of this great luminary.

Equally incredible are the number of attributes the man possessed; each one so lovingly highlighted by this person or that, whether colleague, boss, friend or patient.

"Sexuality education and counselling was his mission, his passion and religion – he was a true *karmayogi*; a workaholic," says Dr. Brahmbhatt about Dr. Watsa.

Whether consciously or unconsciously, whether he was saying it in a literal sense or using it as a metaphor, whatever be the case, but Dr. Brahmbhatt has put his finger on the key to understanding the personality of Dr. Watsa.

He was indeed a *karmayogi*. A man who was focussed on his '*dharma*', that of taking sexuality education to the widest possible audience in order to, through the weapon of knowledge, promote the safety and welfare of adolescents and women; ease sexuality related problems and trauma suffered by persons of all sexes, ages and propensities; and thus to improve the overall health of society. And, like a typical *karmayogi*, he had no thought of reward. His calling was not a business, or even a career pursuit in the traditional sense. It was something which he just felt compelled to do, and he put his whole heart and soul into it.

Dr. Narayana Reddy emphasises: "Dr. Watsa did a lot for the promotion of sexual health education. He was given the recognition he deserved by his colleagues, but the government never recognised his worth. Many doctors who did not do as much, or were not as deserving, got Padma awards, but not him." And this is a grievance of many of his associates.

Dr. Watsa was acknowledged as a great leader by all his colleagues; one who on a single call was able to gather people for whatever task was at hand.

Dr. Reddy points to one quality of Dr. Watsa's which is tough to find in a leader and so eminent a person, but one which no doubt endeared him to his colleagues. "He was a great team player and immensely person-centric," he comments. "Dr. Watsa took everyone on board – and that skill I learnt from him. He would always say: 'If you want to do something good be a team player, not a dictator or individualist'."

He adds: "Though Dr. Watsa was a great leader, he would not have agreed to being called one. Many who practise today consider him to be their mentor."

One facet which was his hallmark was his utter equanimity in the face of all situations. This aspect has been remarked upon by almost everyone.

"Dr. Watsa was always calm, collected, and cool, and extremely reasonable," sums up Dr. Reddy. "In the course of conferences and other discussions, I have seen other people getting agitated and angry – but never Dr. Watsa. Often, he helped calm us all down."

Dr. Soonawala who had the greatest opportunity of seeing him from close quarters over the longest period of time, describes Dr. Watsa as a kind-hearted, soft-spoken, loving individual, who had no enemies but a wide circle of friends from all walks of life.

"He was very soothing, like a father figure; always positive and very calm," he says. "However difficult a problem he was confronted with, he would never get irritated or angry. He was a good mediator if any argument or fight broke out, as he had the ability to inspire confidence in anybody, that this was a man who knows what he is talking about."

This quality of being a caring 'father figure' – oft repeated by many – has touched each and every person he has come in contact with, whether from India, or those from abroad with whom he had worked. The expression of his warm-heartedness covered a range of experiences.

One and all remember the loving concern that not only Dr. Watsa, but even Promila, had for his colleagues and their circle of friends. There are numerous anecdotes and every person of his inner circle has their own bouquet of memories of the incidents which are legion.

Dr. Baam also remarks that he was "like a father figure" for her; and, in fact, he once urged her to find a nice groom because she was still unmarried at 30! "He looked after all his staff very well and played an important role in shaping their careers," she recalls.

Dr. Brahmbhatt says: "We had a father and son relationship – I am grateful to God for giving me the opportunity of interacting and working with a man like him. He gave me everything on a silver platter. He took me into the FPAI; he founded CSEPI and included me as one of the members of the founding board."

Dr. Palarp Sinhaseni was working as an associate dean for research affairs of the Institute of Health Research, Chulalongkorn University, Bangkok, Thailand, when she first met Dr. Watsa many years ago in one of CSEPI's annual conferences in Mumbai. Thereafter, she often attended

CSEPI conferences in various places all over India.

On her first trip to Chennai, she could not get on a booked return Indian Airlines flight and was left alone at a foggy airport. She decided to telephone Dr. Watsa and he told her immediately get on a flight to Mumbai. Only, she had no luggage as it had already been sent to Bangkok.

That unexpected event led to a lifelong and the most precious friendship she says she will always treasure. Promila and Dr. Watsa showed her the true Buddhist "*Kalayanamitra* friendship" – friends who empower you, friends who wish you well; truthful, caring and at all times dependable.

She was always welcome to stay at the Watsa home and was very comfortable in their kitchen as well. She would go to the market with their cook and buy ingredients to cook them a Thai meal on each of her homestays with them.

After Promila's passing, Dr. Watsa even gave Dr. Palarp one of her beautiful necklaces in memory of her which she still treasures.

Dr. Palarp feels grateful and honoured to have known both Promila and Dr. Watsa and says she will always cherish the great memories of all the time spent together with them both.

"Both Prom and Dr. Watsa were my dearest friends," she writes. "I am lucky to have known them."

She thought Dr. Watsa was a very "genuine person". She remembers particularly that he ordered a pack of Alphonso mangoes for her every season!

"Dr. Watsa was a kind and very dependable person," she says. "He excelled in the field he chose – professional counselling."

For Nandini Johri, the concern that Dr. Watsa had for all those around him has left a permanent impression. "Dr. Mahinder Watsa and Mrs. Promila Watsa were always happy to meet the family members of the SECRT staff. They had deep concern for the well-being of the counsellors as well as their family members," she says. "To cite an example: when my father was hospitalised in 2001 and in 2013-14, Dr. Watsa remained in constant touch with me and the concerned doctors over the phone, and helped me maintain my calm and confidence during those trying times."

She feels that Dr. Watsa was such a wonderful person, that whosoever interacted and worked with him, was thoroughly impressed. "There was so much to learn from Dr. Watsa's knowledge and experience. One learnt not only about the subject, but also drew lessons from his behaviour. For example, one learnt about dedication, perseverance, determination; and how to effectively deal with difficult colleagues/participants without getting discouraged, come what may," she elaborates. "Dr. Watsa also utilised time very efficiently. I remember, when we travelled together by train, bus or flight, he would keenly discuss about upcoming project activities, research, report writing etc. to make the best use of time throughout the journey."

She adds: "The immense affection and care that I received from Dr. and Mrs. Watsa for so many years has been an invaluable treasure for me. Hence, even after leaving SECRT in March 2000, when I moved to Seattle in USA for a Fellowship programme (and later joined other organisations), I continued to be Dr. Watsa's disciple."

"Essentially he was a mild man, a tolerant man," emphasises Dr. Vikram Sharma. "He was peaceful, and had a steadiness in him – most people don't have this peace and tolerance. In that sense he was a philosophical man. That made it easy for him to live and let live."

One facet of Dr. Watsa's which was not necessarily widely on display, but has been mentioned by a few colleagues is that he was a very "knowledgeable" man. He kept in touch with a wide array of literature on his subjects and was very aware of the latest developments.

"He was very widely read," affirms Dr. Kalpana Apte. "And the library of FPAI was built up in large measure thanks to him. He was always recommending this or that publication or book be bought for the FPAI library."

"As a doctor he had all the desirable attributes for inspiring confidence: a good bedside manner, he was knowledgeable in his field, and was a patient listener," the late Albert C. de Souza had once shared. "His patients were from across all social strata – from high society ladies to local residents from the sea front."

Pia Barve, a patient as well as a family friend, unfortunately passed away recently, while this book was being prepared for publication. She had earlier spoken to the author, and was a most enthusiastic proponent of Dr. Watsa on all fronts.

"When I got married in 1975 and came to Mumbai, I was introduced to him and from that time he not only became my physician, but my friend, philosopher and guide," she had enthused.

All praise for the manner in which he handled his patients with utmost care and patience, she had said that he would take a lot of time with each one, rarely getting flustered or impatient. She remembered he had this cottage with the huge compound, and wouldn't prevent anyone from coming to his clinic. So at all times there were large crowds of poor people sitting around.

It is obvious that Dr. Watsa was extremely vivid in her mind to the last. Her description of how he spoke would bring him alive to anyone who heard her. "He had this soft way of speaking and would start most dialogues with 'Look here' and then start off to say whatever he was saying," she had said with a laugh.

Narrating one incident, she cited the example of her husband's nephew who had set up a clinic in Chimbai, Bandra in later years: "Uncle Minny would say to me: 'Look here, Dr. Barve has set up a clinic, now you have to go to his clinic; and you must go to Dr. Barve's clinic in your car'. He was saying this so that it would help our nephew get established. He was so caring, that there was no one he was not concerned about."

Pia remarked that Dr. Watsa's geniality and kindness was legendary;

and he was such an upright and honest man, never once taking advantage of any situation.

"When the property (on which his cottage clinic stood) went up for redevelopment, he took just one flat," she had said with amazement in her voice. "When anyone commented that he could have acquired more, he would say 'What do I need more for?' There was no greed in that man. And in the one flat that he got he opened a polyclinic and had a number of doctors associated with it as well as a sonography unit and so on."

As a doctor, Pia remembered that his diagnosis was phenomenally accurate – something that not all doctors can boast about.

"When my mother was very seriously ill, I took him to the hospital," Pia had shared. "And immediately he put his finger on what the problem was – though it was too late by then. His diagnosis was never wrong and he also always had simple prescriptions – he was a doctor of the old school."

Then there was the famous "openness" that one and all talk about; the ability to discuss this difficult subject of sex and sexology without mincing words.

In the famous Pune Conference, Dr. Soonawala remembers, Dr. Watsa asked all the doctors participating to describe male organs. "Most were hesitant and even I was very self-conscious," he laughs. "Yet, that experience made us realise just how little we were used to tackling the subject in a straightforward manner."

Dr. Baam remembers an incident in her early days working with Dr. Watsa, when he was taking a session with young adolescent boys on various family planning methods. The topic under discussion was "How to put on a condom".

She was sitting at the rear end of the auditorium filled with boys, thoroughly embarrassed. Dr. Watsa spoke with such ease and calm, providing simple and lucid explanations without any embarrassment or shame. She was so highly impressed with the session that it gave her the confidence to speak on the same topic going forward.

Dr. Watsa was widely known for his ability to tell it as it was and never use euphemisms. He also put great emphasis on Indianising the dialogue. And he was completely comfortable with people, whether he was speaking in a slum or to the topmost doctors in an air-conditioned five star hotel.

"Firstly, he taught me and people he trained how to be comfortable with themselves as far as sexuality is concerned," elaborates Dr. Brahmbhatt. "He also taught us how to break the ice before an audience – once I was addressing 35 women and I can tell you it was a daunting task. But I did manage to do it."

The gay rights activist Ashok Row Kavi had much opportunity to see this facet of Dr. Watsa as he was a neighbour and family friend of the Watsas. "Dr. Watsa was a very open person. He believed in calling a spade a spade – but was always most dignified," he remembers.

Moreover, it was not just lip service Dr. Watsa paid. "He came with me for the first candle light vigil we held at Dadar when AIDS first hit our shores," Ashok recalls. "When there were things he didn't understand, he was always willing to discuss and listen to another point of view."

He is all admiration for Dr. Watsa's approach to sexual identity. "Most middle class parents of gay and lesbian children ask if there is a 'cure' for their sexual orientation," he says. "Minny was more concerned with 'How do we make them productive, equal members of society?' He helped a lot of people. He would refer them to me if he felt they would benefit from my counselling them."

Another important contribution of Dr. Watsa's was to evolve standards and rules. "The first rule of adult counselling is confidentiality," asserts Ashok. "Minny was the one who set the guidelines and was very strict about them. He was responsible for evolving the Code of Sexuality Counselling on a professional basis."

Hand in hand with these rules – for example he would never counsel a woman patient without another lady being present – was also the matter of his approach to counselling and his patients. It was not at all about preaching or instructing them to do this and that. "Minny was a true counsellor, one who only gives his/her opinion, never pushes in a particular direction," Ashok explains. "He would leave it to you; you must choose the true course as an individual."

Dr. Watsa only drew the line at self harm, harm towards others and domestic violence – he was totally against it and keen to prevent it.

As time went on, he became more and more perplexed about the developments taking place in society around him.

Dr. Suchitra Dalvie who spent a lot of time interacting with, and discussing all sorts of topics – especially in the latter years – remembers that in response to the kind of censorship which was sought to be imposed and the negative reaction to his column, he would sometimes question – "Where are we headed?"

Ashok similarly recalls how disturbed Dr. Watsa was when the Nirbhaya rape incident took place in 2012, and during its aftermath.

"We would have long-ranging discussions when the Nirbhaya incident became public. He was very distressed," Ashok says. "He would keep saying 'I just don't understand it. How can anyone be so bestial?'"

Dr. Malde astutely points out that amongst Dr. Watsa's most significant contributions is the veritable army of sexuality educationists, counsellors and therapists he trained over the years. "Dr. Watsa's main contribution was to create a vast cadre of doctors who believed sexual problems could be treated scientifically – and went on to actually do so," he explains.

There can be no doubt that Dr. Watsa inspired the greatest hero worship amongst all who have been trained by him or worked with him as their boss. Again, like in all things, there were many facets even to this aspect of his character.

"As a boss he was most approachable – he was direct, friendly and he always spoke to people as equals," emphasises Dr. Dalvie.

His two greatest qualities were that he was always supportive and stood behind his staff; and he was always encouraging – for people to learn, grow, take more responsibility; in short, he gave them every opportunity to shine.

Malathi Pillai, who went on to work for international bodies emphasises: "I can say with assurance that I reached where I did because of him."

Dwelling on some of his other qualities she adds: "He was way ahead of his time. He did not mince words and was able to convey what he thought without being impolite."

Dr. Sona Sethi (Rai), who worked with Dr. Watsa for a decade when he was Medical Director at FPAI and she the Assistant Medical Director, makes an interesting observation when she states unequivocally: "FPAI was a pioneer through Dr. Watsa."

For her too, like all the others, his greatest quality was that he was very open – he encouraged people to grow. "I myself owe my growth to him," she affirms. "He made me aware of my strengths."

One incident still remains vividly in her mind. Soon after she joined his department, Dr. Watsa was scheduled to address a meeting of donors, outlining the work of the Medical Department. As he just didn't show up, she was called upon to speak instead, and address the meeting. She was totally unprepared and extremely nervous, as this was the first time she was speaking before a large audience; and, she was fairly new to the department.

However, she managed to do a good job and was appreciated by all. "Even Mrs. Wadia came and said to me: 'Sona you did a great job' and I was so thrilled! Later, when I asked Dr. Watsa why he had not turned up and had thrown me in the water, he simply smiled and said in his typical gentle manner: 'I knew you could do it, so I deliberately stayed away. I wanted you to get the experience.' And I said to myself, 'How blessed am I to have such a mentor!'," she recounts.

She remembers that he was always open to suggestions and his regular response was "OK. Let's try it out".

"Thus, we were able to introduce small changes to improve the quality of care offered at the 43 FPAI clinics, depending on client feedback," she says. "He made people comfortable; discussed serious matters and offered advice in a very non-threatening way. He was the best, most humble boss I have had till today. He was a people's person – everyone just loved him."

As in the case of so many who he worked with, Sona and her husband Narendra, developed a close personal relationship with Dr. Watsa as well as Promila, and were included in their social life too. "She was a person who could scold you while being most affectionate," remembers Sona with a smile about Promila. "She would scold my husband saying – 'Don't smoke'. She helped me pick up antique furniture, and those were some of my most prized possessions. When they came to Bangkok, they stayed with us. Both of them were always very helpful and our friendship continued even after I left the FPAI."

The other aspect of his supportive nature Sona will never forget is her experience when she made the move out of FPAI. She had got to know about an opportunity in CARE when she was still working with Dr. Watsa. She hadn't told anyone, but had gone and appeared for the interview. When she did tell him – a little apprehensively – of what she had done, all he said in his typically softly modulated voice was: "Go Sona. We will all miss you, but you have to grow."

Dr. Dalvie, for her part, remembers a project funded by a small donor she was working on. It was about medical research and the donor's representative was insisting that he wanted to be the writer of the project report.

She went and took up the matter with Dr. Watsa. "He heard me out and asked, 'What do you think about it?'," she recalls. "Now, the person concerned was a very senior, important person and I realised that there might be repercussions. Yet, I expressed my opinion frankly to Dr. Watsa

– that under the Vancouver guidelines one gets authorship only if the aspiring writer fulfills the five points listed under those guidelines – otherwise it would be unethical and inappropriate. I said that FPAI could acknowledge the funding and give the donor credit."

Dr. Watsa was very supportive. He said, "If you think something needs to be done, do it; I am behind you – don't let your creativity and passion be dimmed."

She also recalls that when the organisation was doing its annual planning, he would always advise the staff to make plans in such a way that all work had to be finished in the third quarter. That way, if any hurdles cropped up, they would have a buffer to get the plans implemented – which is sound administrative advice.

His philosophy was always: "Get Things Done". Take risks if you have to, but just get on with it.

The other aspect about him which is memorable, particularly with regard to old organisations which were almost quasi-governmental, is that he was completely unassuming and never stood on ceremony, which was very refreshing. Often, "bosses" and senior executives of such bodies can be extremely hierarchical in outlook and behaviour.

"He would move around the office talking to everyone," Dr. Dalvie recalls. "He would walk into my cabin and say I wanted to talk to you about this or that – when he could easily have called me to him as others would have done. He was a thorough gentleman too."

His ability to get things done, translated in a multitude of situations. Dr. Brahmbhatt recalls an incident when Kevan Wylie, when he was the President of the World Association for Sexual Health (WAS) was in India and was scheduled to visit Willingdon Club with a team as guests of Dr. Watsa. When the group arrived, they found that one of the persons of the visiting delegation was not dressed as per club rules (presumably he was casually dressed in shorts). "So now, they needed to procure a pair of trousers – and the question was where could they get trousers at this short notice?," Dr. Brahmbhatt recounts. "But Watsa was not to be stumped. He went to the Manager of the Club, and requested to borrow a laundered trouser, part of the staff uniform; and did manage to procure one! He was very resourceful like that and could manage to arrange almost anything, anytime."

Dr. Watsa also had an extremely good connect with foreigners, and was able to build up a large network of specialists working in the sexuality education, counselling and therapy field. And even in that he was most thoughtful and warm. "When he was travelling, he would always pack small little gifts which he could give the people he met," remembers Dr. Brahmbhatt. "He was very generous and open-handed: If he found something good, he would always share it."

His generosity, like so many of his other characteristics, is legendary. Dr. Jha remembers she was meeting him one day before Covid struck, when he suddenly said to her. "I found some plates in a shop, they are very nice. Take six." When she declined, he insisted saying that he didn't need them and so she should take them. "I asked why then, had he purchased them? He told me, 'I liked them so I bought them. I also like to give things away'! He was always extremely generous – when he was at Willingdon with friends, he would often say – why don't you go and pick up something at the shop? He always wanted to give things to people."

In fact, so generous was he, and so widely did he give of his worldly goods, that the family has lost count of what all and how much has been given away.

This "giving away" is again a quality of the *karmayogi* – not interested in gathering the fruits of his labour or in material things, but only in the *karma*, the action itself. "He was always giving, always giving," emphasises Trishla. "He was not like one of these commercial-minded doctors, not a materialistic person at all – he was not doing it for money – he always just wanted to help people, that's all."

Again, as in all things, almost every colleague will no doubt have their own "travel story" of Dr. Watsa.

Dr. Soonawala has quite a few, being one of those associated with Dr. Watsa, over such a long period. "There are a few occasions on our various trips together, which I still remember vividly," he says thoughtfully. "When he joined FPAI we had the opportunity of travelling together to Iran, and had a long transit stop in Jalandhar and we decided to accompany him to his ancestral home in the city, occupied by another family. He bore no resentment, only had genuine joy in seeing that it was still being used as a family home, albeit by someone unknown to him."

"On another occasion we were travelling for a lecture at Banaras Hindu University and our car broke down," he recounts. "Two of us from the group were most upset and worried that we would be late for the lecture. Minny calmly hailed a cycle-rickshaw and the three of us sat in it and this really thin and puny cycle-rickshawalla was slowly pedalling us along towards the lecture venue. All the while Minny was serenely enjoying the leisurely ride which allowed him to take in the sights and sounds and smells of the city – until we met up with another car which had been sent to fetch us, and we managed to reach the lecture in time!"

Then again, he adds one more story saying: "Once we got late for a flight to Guwahati from Calcutta (Kolkata), not realising that eastern India in those days had a different time zone. My brother Fardoon and I had to make use of our years of athletic training, and run across the tarmac to get to the boarding ladder of the plane. What surprised us was not only had Minny reached before us, but was breathing completely normally, while the two of us national level sprinters were breathless and arrived second!"

Dr. Brahmbhatt tells of a time when they were returning in a group from a conference. "We were coming back from Jabalpur and the train stopped at Igatpuri," he says. "One of the doctors on the group was nervous about getting back, so in order to distract him and put him at ease, Dr. Watsa said, 'Lets plan next year's conference'. And before we knew it, we were in deep discussion and the tension had eased."

Acknowledging the many learnings from his interaction with Dr. Watsa, he says: "I could do everything I did because of my training from him." A view echoed by all his juniors who became his colleagues.

Dr. Watsa was seen as a workaholic by many, and he spent a lot of time and energy on his work. Dr. Brahmbhatt says he was like the rock of Gibraltar – he knew everything.

Moreover, as Dr. Brahmbhatt remarks, "He was not one for sitting on his laurels – he was always moving to the next thing."

Trishla Jain talks about how he was a workaholic till the end; and how passionate he was about his chosen field – sexology. Often, he would get up at 4 am to check his e-mails and to begin preparing answers to them.

That had been his trajectory since the beginning, as all his colleagues know. When there was work to be done, he was completely absorbed and gave it his 100 per cent.

Yet, Dr. Watsa was by no means a dull boy. So, it was certainly not a question of all work and no play. As all his closest friends and colleagues will tell you, once work was done, he liked nothing better than to gather his friends around him and entertain people individually or in small groups or sometimes even party away in large gatherings – whether at home in Mumbai or when he was travelling to some other place for conferences or meetings.

"During working hours, we worked very hard and with great focus – after that we enjoyed our leisure time to the hilt too," remarks Dr. Brahmbhatt. "When he was relaxing it was like we were 18 years old. Dr. Watsa lived life kingsize."

"He was a very lively person," Dr. Reddy recalls. "I used to stay with him whenever I was in Mumbai – not that FPAI would not have put me up at a hotel – but this way we could spend more time together. Sometimes in the evenings, we would watch Hollywood movies – he was a highly westernised man, very exposed to western thought and culture."

"We were a great combination and had a great rapport," he says looking back with nostalgia.

Dr. Sharma echoes Dr. Reddy's view of Dr. Watsa as a citizen of the world and his "universal"outlook. "Watsa never had a local orientation," he expounds. "Maybe because his father was in the army and he had attended so many schools and also been out of the country on his father's postings. He was more like an Indian – not 'I am a Punjabi' kind of person."

Highlighting his social nature, the late Albert C. de Souza had said: "Any observation on Dr. Watsa would be incomplete if I did not mention that he led a hectic social life. We often wondered how he found the time to be a doctor, manager, advisor and meet people. He was a compulsively friendly, people's man. Over the years my wife and I must have shared his excellent table innumerable times. His wife and he were the perfect hosts."

Not only did he socialise widely and often, organising many parties, he took a special joy in his own birthday celebrations, be they big or small, which his family and friends would organise for him.

If he was a father figure to all, and everyone looked up to him as a wise confidante and counsellor, in this one aspect – the pleasure in celebrating his own birthday – he displayed an almost childlike quality.

Trishla remembers the first birthday after she joined him full time as an Assistant – though she had known him virtually since her birth as the two families were close friends over a couple of generations; and he was present at her birth at the insistence of her grandmother. Besides, she had spent a few years helping part time with various communications related jobs. So, she was familiar with the household, the office staff and their routine.

On that particular day, everyone went about their work without referring to it being a special day in anyway. "No one wished him, no one said anything to him. Arati (his help) had prepared some special snacks but we went about pretending that it was just another day. Actually, we were all waiting for Ayesha (his granddaughter). We could see that he was getting puzzled and the questions were building up inside him. Finally, he could contain himself no longer and he said addressing us – 'You know it's my birthday?'."

His family and some friends recall how even when he was at the Breach Candy Hospital HDU, as he was recovering from an attack of double pneumonia, in 2019, they celebrated his 95th birthday at his bedside. Yet, despite it all, he was still at his sparkling best – and could well have matched the brightness of the candles on the cake he cut. In fact, he cut two cakes in the presence of Dr. Baam and some other colleagues. "Even at that age of 95, he charmed all the nurses in the HDU and they all rallied around him as he cut his two cakes," she recalls.

Only five years previously, his friends had come together to celebrate a milestone birthday – his 90th. The organising of this one was entrusted to Dr. Sharma and a few others. "I also organised a few games with Trishla's help," he says. "One of them was 'Bombay Calling' – it was great fun, as we had made up some clues and the guests had to guess which Mumbai place/monument it was. As I recall, Dr. Dalvie won that one. Then we had a sing song session. All in all we had a great party."

The last birthday – Dr. Watsa's 96th – was celebrated in February 2020 at Willingdon Club with family and a few friends. Even then, he was extremely kind and generosity personified.

After the party, Dr. Baam and her husband, Dr. Rusi Baam, were waiting for a cab. Dr. Watsa was with his sister Sheila Khanna who had specially come down from Delhi for his birthday; he immediately invited the Baams to get into the car and insisted on dropping them home first.

Soon after that, Covid, which had already swept through a large part of the world arrived in India. The rest is history. Dr. Watsa never made it to his 97th.

But no description of Dr. Watsa would be complete without mention of what amounted to his passion for food. He loved food with a rare heartiness and spent many happy times in its pursuit.

"Dr. Watsa loved to eat," Pia had said. She, incidentally, was herself a food specialist, running a catering business; and had shared his love of culinary delights. "We would exchange notes on which was the best place to get what dish – and then he would go off and buy it," she had remembered with delight. "This would irritate Aunty Promila as he was always going off and buying something or the other! He loved pork chops, prawn curry rice – we had found a place where you could get it for Rs. 18 – he loved different kinds of food. Chocolate cake was one of his favourites – he simply loved it, even till the last."

In fact, recounts Trishla, he was extremely fond of sweets – *puranpoli* was another favourite; and he also loved ice cream and chocolates.

Dr. Jha remembers that the two-three times she went to visit him just before the lockdown and would ask him if she could get him something, he always chose food – something like butter chicken. "He was a great foodie," she chuckles.

"After Promila passed away, and as he grew older, he found that Indira and I were people he could talk to without reservation – he nicknamed us the Trinity and we would meet at least once a month and later at least once in three months," she recalls.

Dr. Dalvie who also visited him regularly in the last years, says he was a very interesting person with very eclectic friends and very solicitous towards all. "He was always planning dinners and lunches with close colleagues and friends."

"In my long years of association and friendship with Dr. Watsa, we often met over a meal in Mumbai or in Delhi and chatted over matters other than professional, enjoying a tasty dish of pomfret, roast chicken and sometimes Chinese food," recalls Nina Puri, former President of FPAI. "Indeed, he was very discerning about cuisine and had once mentioned in passing that at one point of time he had even considered becoming a chef! Very impishly he remarked 'I make very good ice cream'."

Moving on to another aspect, Trishla comments: "The beauty of Dada (as he was called by his family and a wider circle of those close to him) was that he always looked at a problem from a woman's point of view. He was a thorough liberal and very ahead of his times."

The natural ability to see things from the women's viewpoint was uniquely his own, and remarked upon and appreciated by all – his patients, colleagues and friends alike.

There were several cases of domestic violence that he encountered, and he would always tell the ladies to stand up for themselves. When one of his patients came to him alone one day and said to him "Why don't you do something?", he is said to have told her that whatever had to be done had to be done by her. "You should stand up against him (her husband who was abusing her physically) and not allow him to beat you," he is supposed to have told his patient. And from that day, she stood up to her husband and never had a problem again.

His practice included a large number of women as he had developed a reputation of understanding women and could see things from their point of view. To a woman at the receiving end of male chauvinism and patriarchal arrogance, his soft sympathetic nature must have been akin to manna from heaven – his clinic, a veritable haven.

Trishla remembers how the fisherfolk from Uttan who loved him would come to his house even in the later years, early in the morning and sit in the balcony. "And it was not one or two families, it was like they got the whole *gaon* with them," she laughs.

"Dada was a living legend, a doctor par excellence," she sums up. "He wasn't a commercial doctor but was someone who was driven by his love and passion for his work. But more than that he was a very, very fine human being and that is what truly made him such a wonderful doctor/counsellor. He was a rare gem of a person – humble, loving, caring, understanding, kind, compassionate, benevolent, a very giving person, always smiling, a thorough gentleman. He had the knack of befriending people of any age and making them feel comfortable."

Terming his demise as an irreparable loss, she says: "To me he was a father figure. I have lost my best friend, confidant and guide."

The praise of Aavabai Wadia, permanently etched in the pages of her book, rings out proclaiming Dr. Watsa's contribution. "In Bombay we had an expert counsellor in Dr. Mahinder Watsa who had the vision and drive to go further to assemble a professional team of doctors and counsellors to work in different parts of the country," she wrote.

Pia had summed up his personality saying: "He was a big man, a strapping man – he took up space both due to his physique, and as much due to his personality. He was an amazing man, his magnanimity was something else – his heart, his philosophy, his aura, were all very special."

Dr. Brahmbhatt adds: "He had great charisma – he would literally glow. When he died it was truly the end of an era. Thousands of years pass before such a man is born."

To Dr. Dalvie "He was like a colossus who strides though the decade."

His very special contribution is succinctly pinpointed by Dr. Rusi Soonawala when he says: "His charming manner and ability to break barriers opened the public's mind to the fact that sex is not something dirty and not to be discussed at all. In my opinion, this would probably be one of his greatest and everlasting contributions to Indian society. He was, in a true sense, larger than life – the man of the century where sexual medicine is concerned."

Dr. Reddy echoes the thoughts of the community when he says: "He should be recognised at least posthumously."

SOMETHING FOR EVERYONE -1

The 2015 published It's Normal! *(expounded upon in the previous chapter) is a mini compendium of Watsa thought. Mini, because, as he said in the Preface: "It would not do justice to the subject to try and discuss all the problems that I have come across; rather, I have picked only those that worry people the most."*

Excerpts from the book:

BEING COMFORTABLE WITH SEX

'Sex is Religion, Sex is Philosophy, Sex is Ethics, Sex is Science, and Sex is Human Existence'

An inscription at the entrance of a Shinto shrine in Japan

WHAT IS SEX?

"Sex is an aid to happiness and work, a substitute for all manner of drugs and a healer of many sorts of sicknesses. Sex is for fun, pleasure and ecstasy. It binds people together with cords of romance, gratitude and love. It produces children. Sex is also about attitudes, values and responsibilities."

'A healthy mind in a healthy body' is the basis for good sex. Sexual attitudes, beliefs, values, environment and responsibilities must form the platform for your sexual behaviour, positive thinking will always translate into positive sexual feelings.

Many of the problems with love and sex that we encounter in our lives are rooted in misinformation and the lack of knowledge, understanding or communication. We often pick up confusing messages about sex during childhood or adolescene, for example, 'Masturbation can harm the body'.

The key to being comfortable with sex and sexuality is feeling good about yourself, understanding how your body works, having knowledge of sexual techniques and receiving care and respect from your partner.

Understanding yourself is important - your sexuality, by which we mean what you like about sex, what turns you on and how you feel about yourself. The sex act is physical but your sexuality is largely emotional and intellectual.

The first essential in improving your sex life is making enough time for it.

Your lifestyle is in your hands. Smoking and chewing paan (betel leaves) with tobacco and lime can be detrimental to health. Take alcohol if you must, but only on social occasions, and it will not harm you, but it is easy to step over the line and that can lead to consequences. Saying no or knowing how much is enough is not easy to learn, but you must practise it to ensure a healthy sexual life.

Meditation helps to keep anxiety, tension and stress under control.

For the ageing, cultivating an optimistic self-image, staying fit and healthy and maintaining a positive attitude during mid-life can effectively counter many of the problems that arise.

Physical fitness is important. The less fit you are, the less comfortable you will be sexually. Daily exercise is a must; brisk walking is recommended and yoga is particularly useful. Such activities will ensure good stamina and keep your weight under control. Eating regular home-cooked food and minimising the intake of junk food will keep you sexually fit. Prayer and meditation can calm a turbulent mind.

QUESTIONS

Q. *What should one expect from sex? Should it be a constant ringing of bells, flashing of lights and fireworks, all thickly layered with passionate declarations of love?*

A NO. Try for a sex life that is emotionally and physically fulfilling because it is ever-changing. Cosy and gentle when you need it to be cosy and gentle; passionate and high-voltage when you need it to be passionate and high-voltage; exotic and adventurous when you need it to be exotic and adventurous.

Q. *Many people get extremely anxious and feel guilty if they have thoughts which they consider 'bad'.*

A The wonderful thing about sexual fantasies is that you can have them any way you like. As an accompaniment to masturbation, sexual fantasies can be marvellously effective for increasing arousal. In short, everything sexual that you have ever wanted or wondered about can be yours through the magic of fantasy. In our fantasies we frequently perform actions that we would never dream of doing in real life.

Q. *What is the basis of or reason for female sexual problems?*

A Women go through several traumatic situations in life

1. At birth – instant dislike/disappointment of parents – communicated by unspoken words and overt action.
2. Around five years – preferential treatment – develop penis envy (Freud).
3. Adolescence – acute anguish and anxiety regarding

body image - height, pimples, breasts - dejected if rejected.
4. Menstruation - could be a memorable or traumatic experience.
5. First night - fear and dislike of the act (rape by the man) - trauma - painful sex (vaginismus).
6. Loss of expectations from partner.
7. Unwanted pregnancy.
8. Feeling of being used by partner (receptacle for his semen).
9. Menopause or change of life.
10. Old age - rejection - loss of prestige.

Sex education can be harmful when the girl is educated and the man is not. It could lead to misunderstandings when the wife takes the lead. Most sexual problems in females are caused by males. Women often feel hurt and unfulfilled but seldom express it openly.

Q. *How frequently should one visit a sexologist? The same as a dentist – once in six months? Is there a set of regular check-ups that one needs to get done once a year?*

A Fortunately, the penis does not have toothaches. You can check your penis - does the foreskin slip back easily, do you notice any changes in the testicles, are your libido and erection good? As for women, they should visit their gynaecologist once a year.

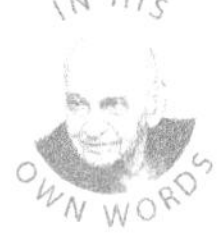

CHAPTER 10

THE SEXPERT AS A FAMILY MAN

1924-2020

Birth, living, and death. The eternal circle of life. In the course of completing this arc, a large part of humanity follows a set pattern. One is born; one grows up, gets educated – or not; makes a living one way or the other; and many go on to establish a family with partner and offspring – and generally go on to lead ordinary, everyday lives. Others blaze trails, lead exceptional, extraordinary lives and are remembered. Yet, most are touched, and enveloped by family one way or the other. For better or for worse.

Family, which can be both anchor and harbour for its members. Family, which has been called a life jacket in stormy seas by author J.K. Rowling.

Blessed are those for whom it is a bulwark, support and source of encouragement; and woe is the lot of those for whom it is a weighty millstone round their neck. A man with abilities and skills who is lucky enough to fall in the former category is capable of soaring high and touching the skies.

"Let there be spaces in your togetherness,
And let the winds of the heavens dance between you.
Love one another, but make not a bond of love:
Let it rather be a moving sea between the
shores of your souls."

Kahlil Gibran
Writer & Poet

The path of a *karmayogi* is not an easy one. It involves complete dedication and immersion in the work one is devoted to. Needless to say, if this committed soul has a family, they are subject to all the consequences that go with being the closest to the *karmayogi*.

Dr. Mahinder C. Watsa was extremely fortunate in the family that came to be his lot. As a young man when he was pursuing Promila he may not have looked so far ahead as the five-and-a-half decades they spent together as man and wife. But it proved to be the ideal choice, and the ideal match, in every which way.

This is amply borne out in the reminiscences of all of Dr. Watsa's closest circle. "Promila and Dr. Watsa were a very loving couple – when I look back, I see a lot of love," says Ashok Row Kavi voicing the sentiment of so many of Dr. Watsa's colleagues and friends.

His words are echoed by Dr. Indira Kapoor. "Minny and Promila were a very happy, loving couple," she emphasises. "They were married for 55 years."

Much of the stability, contentment and happiness within their relationship was due, in no small measure, to the mettle Promila was made of, no doubt. For, wonderful as he was as a human being, doctor and pioneer, a wife with a more demanding nature would have ruined the equation: not only causing unhappiness within the family, but also making it difficult for him to devote his full attention to the work, the cause, he had undertaken. One of Promila's greatest attributes was the absolute devotion she had for her *"Janaab"* as she fondly called Dr. Watsa, and the active support she extended to his work and all that he did.

"Mom was very involved in his conferences – she would always help out with the backend, with the dinners and so on," remembers Gautam. "She also travelled a lot with Dad."

Given that she came from so much affluence, she was a simple woman – though always immaculately turned out – and content enough to live with Dr. Watsa from the first days, wherever life took him.

"She lived happily in this one room which was allotted to Dad as his quarters when he first started out in his career," says Gautam. "And was prepared to travel by bus after she was advised not to drive – she never complained."

A fearless woman, she was never afraid and would drive even at 2 am in the morning if need be.

Promila had a special love of antique furniture and was a regular at the Oshiwara furniture market in Jogeshwari and other old furniture haunts. She took many people – including colleagues and work friends of Dr. Watsa – for shopping, or simply window shopping, to these places.

"She knew all the store owners in the Oshiwara market for antique and replicated antique furniture – long before many people had even heard of the place," comments Gautam.

Most importantly, she had an eye for what was aesthetic. Being no snooty collector, she was happy to acquire pieces with no special provenance, and howsoever humble be their origins as long as they were beautiful – and she always homed in on the best.

Gautam remembers a particular purchase, many years back. In those days, Dr. Watsa was a consultant at Modern Nursing Home near Dadar station; and Promila would often pick him up from there, once his work was done. On the pavement in front of the nursing home there were vendors selling several sundry products. "One of the vendors had this really old rosewood temple which immediately caught my mother's eye. She bought it for just Rs. 100. My aunt loved the temple and got a replica of it made for herself. This rosewood temple occupies a prime spot in our home, even today," says Gautam.

"My mother was very easy-going and rarely lost her cool," avers Gautam. "But she was a very emotional person too, and there were things that would upset her sometimes."

It was fortunate that Promila was so even-tempered. Her patience and serenity were no doubt tested again and again by our *karmayogi*, for once he got involved in work, everything else receded into the background for the time being.

"My father was very absent-minded," smiles Gautam thinking back. "He was invariably late for all the parties Mom and Dad had to attend. At times he would have forgotten about the engagement and at other times he was too busy at work and would tell her to go ahead and he would follow. This became a way of life for my mother and after the initial years, she took it in her stride."

Gautam adds: "On other occasions, he would suddenly say I have five people coming for dinner – at virtually no notice!"

Fortunately, Promila was a great hostess – as well as a consummate cook – and always rose to the occasion and never lost her equanimity.

"My mother was a wonderful cook and made great pork chops or a mutton stew; mixed grill, lemon soufflé, amongst all the other delicious fare she produced," shares Gautam about her most lip-smacking dishes. "She had a big book of recipes she had compiled over the years, which my father simply gave away. He was like that – generous to a fault, and ready to give away anything and everything to anyone who asked."

Gautam was born a few years after his parents were married, when the young Dr. Watsa was just setting out in his career.

"Dad was so busy with not only work and delivering babies but was also involved in a lot of extracurricular activities as well in Medical College," Gautam says. "The day I was born was the day of the Annual Medical Ball, a huge event organised by Dad. I chose that very day to make my entry into the world. I was told later that he just about made it in the nick of time for my birth. My mother would have never forgiven him if he had arrived at the hospital after I was born!"

One attribute husband and wife shared in common was that they were both always prepared to come to the aid of anyone who needed help.

In Dr. Watsa's case he was also constantly advising women to come into their own as well. "He would be continuously encouraging the ladies to stand up for themselves," remembers Gautam. "Perhaps that is why a lot of women would come to him for consultation. They knew that he understood their problems."

This empathy and sympathy for womankind and all the troubles they faced that was intrinsic to Dr. Watsa's nature has been commented upon by all those associated with him, as touched upon earlier.

"As a child, in my growing years, I have vivid memories of Dad leaving home in the morning, sometimes even before I woke up and I was lucky if I saw him back home before 10.30 pm each night," recalls Gautam wistfully. "In my young days when children normally go to bed early, I would stay awake to see Dad, even if it was for just a few minutes. I didn't get to eat dinner with him on most days until I was much older and my bedtime was later. I believe that is the main reason I was not inclined to take up medicine although in the later years I sometimes did have regrets on that front."

Yet, these were only ever passing pangs, momentary flickers. The doubts remained. "When my daughter, Leisha, said at the age of eight she would like to do medicine, Deepa encouraged her to go ahead but I was not at all in favour," Gautam confesses. "After much persuasion she agreed to switch to doing dentistry which she said would allow her the flexibility to keep her hours depending on her family situation."

As far as Dr. Watsa went, absent-mindedness seemed to be a thread, woven through the fabric of the full tapestry of his personal life; though he was absolutely all there in his professional one.

"Dad was always very forgetful even when I was a little boy," recounts Gautam. "During those years we were living in Bandra and I attended Bombay Scottish School. On the days I played games, he was supposed to fetch me from my school. He would invariably have at least three to four people in the car with him, and would be so busy discussing something with them that, as a result, he often drove past me standing on the road waving frantically at him to attract his attention. Despite this quality of absent-mindedness, however, he had such an endearing way about him that you just could not be upset with him for long."

Gautam recalls some more amusing instances. As all the members of the family were fond of dogs, one day, Dr. Watsa decided to bring home a pup. After returning home, it only dawned on him a couple of hours later that he had brought a pup back with him and that it needed to be fed. But the little mite was nowhere to be seen or heard.

"He came out of the bedroom and repeatedly asked Mom and me where the pup was," smiles Gautam at the memory. "Neither of us having seen the pup nor heard him, we thought he was dreaming. He was absolutely sure he had brought home a pup; so surely this little live ball of fur could not have vanished into thin air?! After much searching the house – in vain, I might add – he suddenly remembered he had left the pup in the car! The poor little thing was so frightened when we finally found him crouched under the front car seat. Soon Tipsy, though a Pomeranian, became the mascot and guard dog for my mother."

The second incident involved Dr. Reddy and it occurred way before the cell phone era. Dr. Reddy, who had come to Mumbai from his home base Chennai for an FPAI conference, was a house guest with the Watsas for the duration of the conference.

"Both Dad and Dr. Reddy had driven in Dad's car to the meeting at the FPAI office at Nariman Point," Gautam narrates. "Needless to say, Dad had forgotten that he had taken his car and also Dr. Reddy with him in the car! Once the conference for the day was over, he bid goodbye to everyone, hailed a taxi and headed to Bandra to his clinic. When he reached Chowpatty, it suddenly dawned on him that he had left Dr. Reddy at the venue! He instructed the taxi driver to take an about turn and head back to Nariman Point where Dr. Reddy was frantically looking for him. A relieved Dr. Reddy saw Dad who was gesturing for him to get into the taxi so they could hurry back.

"Dr. Reddy couldn't understand why Dad was in a taxi when they had driven to the venue in his car in the morning. So, when Dr. Reddy was able to get Dad to stop the taxi he asked him why he was taking a taxi when they had driven to the venue in the morning. Only then did Dad remember that he had taken his car! After much coaxing and cajoling the taxi driver – who had thought he had got himself a nice long distance fare – Dad managed to pay him off, and the two finally drove back in the car."

Despite everything, Dr. Watsa did manage to squeeze in some leisure hours and fun times with his family. "Most Sundays if he didn't have any babies to deliver, were reserved for family picnics," Gautam remembers. "There were two other families who were close family friends. So the Kamtes, the Kinis and the Watsas would go off on picnics. The job of organising the food would be given to Dad, a complete foodie, and Vasant Uncle (Kamte), who was another foodie. They would leave home with one tiffin box and almost always come back with three tiffins. In one such instance, as usual, they took one tiffin box and, in their enthusiasm, brought back someone else's tiffin box which obviously didn't have the food the three families liked. Imagine the mayhem when all hell broke loose and they got fired by their respective wives!"

Talking of Dr. Watsa's love for food, Gautam relates another incident recounted to him by Dr. Watsa's younger brother, the late Rajin Wats. "Dad was in Calcutta and was assisting Rajin chacha on a surgery," says Gautam. "By the time they finished, it was the early hours of a rainy and foggy morning. They were driving home, when Dad suddenly yelled at Rajin to stop the car. Rajin chacha thought he had run over something. Dad rolled down the window, stuck his nose out and told him to go left and then further, making him stop now and again. They finally reached the destination he wanted to go to – the bakery. He had smelt fresh bread being baked! So sharp was his nose for good food."

In the period that Dr. Watsa worked with Glaxo, he travelled for extensive periods. When Gautam was older, and Dr. Watsa's travel stretched to more than two weeks, Promila would invariably accompany him. On such occasions, Gautam would stay back at home with the staff, as it was more convenient for his journey to school; and his maternal grandparents would look in on him twice a day.

"For me, sex education started at a very early age," remembers Gautam. "I remember being called to Eros Cinema to watch movies made by WHO on sex education and then being questioned on what I saw and understood."

Diametrically opposite to the plain talking Watsa household, was the family of Deepa Vaswani, the lady who was destined to be Gautam's wife and Dr. Watsa's *bahu.*

After Dr. Watsa's passing, she was completely overcome. "There is so much I want to say that I don't know where to begin," she says mournfully. "It's not very often that I am at a loss for words but I can truly say this one time, where do I begin?"

In her case, the beginning of her interaction with her future father-in-law was sought to be a casual encounter. "I recall meeting Dad way back in the early '70s when Gautam and I started dating," she remembers. "Dad had undergone a surgery at Breach Candy Hospital. I had gone to the hospital to see him and taken a bouquet of flowers for him. I was introduced to him as Gautam's friend but he had such a knowing look on his face. He was an absolute charmer even then."

So, though she had met Dr. Watsa occasionally while she was dating Gautam, it was not very often – for he was invariably away at work when she visited the house – and nor had the two conversed for any length of time when they did meet. One day, just a few days before Gautam's and Deepa's wedding, she and Dr. Watsa happened to be sitting in the living room on their own, having a general chat.

"Suddenly, out of the blue, he said to me with a real straight face, with not a hint of any embarrassment on it: 'Now that you are getting married in eight days, have you thought of what method of contraception you are going to use?'" recounts Deepa of her first encounter of Dr. Watsa's plain speaking ways. "Whilst I didn't come from a conservative family, I was certainly not used to discussing these matters with my parents. Here was my to be father-in-law asking me this question. I was caught totally unawares and didn't know where to look. He was not going to let it pass and awaited my response. I remember I looked him straight in the eye and said "Maybe you should ask your son this question". I am not sure he expected this response from me so he let the moment pass. Fortunately, within the next few minutes Gautam and my mother-in-law appeared and we all left together for dinner.

"Later on that evening when Gautam and I got a few minutes alone, I said to him 'Your dad really put me in a very tight spot by asking me this awkward question'." Gautam's laconic response was 'Don't worry you will get used to this in no time'."

Getting "used to it" took some doing – and obviously some time. "The first night back after our honeymoon at the dinner table there was some talk about sex, premature ejaculation etc," remembers Deepa. "I nearly choked on my food and broke out into a coughing spasm. Of course, neither Dad, Mama nor Gautam could understand this sudden coughing fit and everyone rushed to offer me water, was patting my back and so on until I said to them I am not used to this kind of conversation at meal times or any other time either."

After all, conversations at meal times at her parental home had centred around more routine and uncontentious topics like how everyone's day had been and so on. "For me, the Watsa household represented a huge paradigm shift and I was even beginning to wonder if I had made the right choice in choosing my spouse," she says. "However, I have to say, it didn't take me too long to adjust to the new dining table conversations. We also did have "normal" conversations at the dining table but those were few and far between!"

Soon Dr. Watsa was to prove his maverick nature once again – this time in a wholly different direction; one, moreover, that was to seal the growing bond between Deepa and her father-in-law. For, very quickly she had begun to have a real respect and affection for both her in-laws, which is so evident even today when she speaks of either of them.

It came about this way. She had just delivered her elder daughter Ayesha, to the jubilation of all at home. As everyone knows, the first few months of motherhood can be quite a challenge. New mothers are generally always exhausted as they are dealing with entirely new routines and problems. This is when Dr. Watsa's sterling character shone through once again, and he proved that the principles he espoused were not mere words but that he also lived by them.

"Dad knew that I needed and loved my morning sleep; while he was an early riser," Deepa recounts. "Every morning around 5.30 am he would knock on our door and take charge of Ayesha right through till 9 am on most days. He would change her diaper, give her the first bottle feed of the day, and take her for a morning walk in her pram every single day when he was not travelling." How many fathers-in-law would do the same?

That was not all. Deepa adds: "Unfortunately, Ayesha had a lot of health issues but Dad was with us at every doctor's appointment, despite his extremely hectic schedule." From the outset, Dr. Watsa shared a very special bond with his first-born grandchild.

After her extended maternity leave was over, Deepa resumed work; and he continued the morning ritual with Ayesha right through till she was over a year old. "Later, Mama would take over looking after Ayesha with the help of a maid till I got back from the office in the evening," Deepa says.

His solicitous attitude to Deepa continued even after she had resumed work. "My office was at Horniman Circle," Deepa narrates. "Dad used to go to the FPAI office at Nariman Point three times a week: Mondays, Wednesdays and Fridays. Those days he would insist I take a ride back with him in the car instead of taking my contract bus home. He would then drop me home and proceed to his clinic at Hill Road. The ride home with him was always fun as there were invariably several of his lady colleagues from FPAI also taking a ride home with him."

By all calculations, the journey in a private car, even in the 1980s, should have been accomplished faster than the contract bus. Invariably, however, the ride actually took much longer! And what was the delay due to? No prizes for guessing that the culprit causing the delay was the other – apart from Promila, his family and his work – constant love of his life: food!

"We made multiple stops on our way home," laughs Deepa. "The first stop would be at Babulnath to buy something or the other from Dave Farsan: one day it was *farsan*, on another day *kalakand* and so on. The next stop, after dropping off his colleague at Worli Sea Face – or, at times, even before dropping her off – was at the Aarey stall, to have different flavours of Energee. The third stop was at Brijwasi at Worli to get their *boondi laddoos* or some other *mithai*. *Boondi laddoos* were his favourite and remained so right through to the end. The last stop before reaching home was at Manhar Stores at Shivaji Park, just before our house."

Much as she loved the company, the multiple stops and consuming all the goodies, she was very anxious to get home at the earliest to see

Ayesha. "Each time I threatened to take the contract bus home, Dad would promise me that we would drive straight home after fetching me from my office," Deepa says. "I should have known better. He kept his word one time and then instead of four food stops *en route* he would make three! Food and he could never be parted. Gautam has inherited the same trait from his father. Eventually, I relented and look back to those days very fondly now."

Deepa says, voice tinged with nostalgia: "He spoilt me thoroughly every step of the way and treated me like a daughter, never like a daughter-in-law. He always took my side if Gautam and I argued over anything. This was the man I am so very proud to call my father-in-law."

In November 1987, Gautam and Deepa and their by then two daughters moved out of Shivaji Park to their own apartment.

Deepa's last two jobs involved a lot of travel, both international and domestic. Wherever she went, she always remembered to bring back goodies for Dr. Watsa. "His love for sweets knew no bounds," she chuckles. "My return from domestic travel always meant I would stop off at Shivaji Park on the way home to give him his booty. Mama would always tell me I spoiled him with so many sweets! The advent of the sea link, which was the route I began taking, meant I would by-pass Shivaji Park. Though he understood that taking the sea link would save me a lot of time getting home, he was not very happy about it!"

Promila herself had pampered him thoroughly, feels the family, right to the extent of doing his packing for him each time he travelled. When *Janaab* was travelling, Promila would start organising his clothes two to three days prior to his travel to avoid any last minute surprises from him, saying he wanted to carry gifts for whoever he was going to meet and so on. "She would also stick a list of what she had packed on the inside of the suitcase," remembers Deepa fondly.

When Promila passed away in December, 2006, Deepa says Dr. Watsa was quite lost. "It took a little while for him to adjust to life without her but he managed very well eventually," she observes.

He didn't have to worry about running the house, cooking etc, as they had a maid who had been with them for several years and she took over complete charge of everything. What he found most difficult was to pack when he was travelling. "I offered him a simple solution," Deepa says. "I asked him to start with his ticket, hotel booking confirmation, wallet, toilet bag and then work his way up starting from shoes, socks, trousers, hankies and so on, which he found very useful. Lest he forget, I had written this on a post-it and stuck it on his cupboard. It worked and all was well as far as the packing for trips went!"

"What is remarkable is that despite his hectic schedule and his general absent-mindedness, he rarely forgot any of our special occasions," adds Deepa. "He made all of us feel very special on our birthdays and anniversaries with his beautifully hand-written thoughtful notes. We have treasured each of those beautiful messages written by him."

The warm interaction between father-in-law and daughter-in-law had its cute moments too. "I had a very demanding job and travelled extensively every month," says Deepa. "He often felt I was overdoing it, at the same time not accepting that his schedule was far more gruelling than mine ever was. There was one question he would ask me repeatedly every two years. "When will you slow down your pace and retire?" My standard reply to him was "when you slow down, I will consider retiring." I retired when I turned 60 way back in 2013 but he never slowed down. He worked till the very end." By the time Dr. Watsa celebrated his 95th birthday on February 11, 2019 his family had expanded as the granddaughters were grown up; the younger was married to Dean Gomes and also had a bonny baby boy called Mikhail.

Leisha, Dr. Watsa's younger granddaughter, today a successful dentist, expressed her dilemma after his passing, saying: "As his granddaughter, what does one say about the formidable Dr. Watsa? To the world, he was a renowned sexologist, counsellor and columnist extraordinaire, but to me he was just good old Dada.

"The man who would feed the dog despite me saying not to, who made me ice cream growing up even with his crazy schedule, the man who wrote you the most beautiful notes on birthdays (I have every one of them) and the man who until the day he died never really let on how famous he truly was!" She is all admiration for her grandfather as, applauding his immense energy, she says, "He slowed down physically only after he became 96 years old and during the Covid pandemic. Till the lockdown, he was still seeing patients."

Leisha is also astounded by how much of a cross section of society his patients represented. "His patients were very, very diverse – across classes, religions, economic status – and they came for all kinds of issues," she elaborates.

Leisha is also touched by the veneration with which they treated him. "I remember one patient would come from another state only so that Dada could pat his head and say that he was alright," she says admiringly. "That is the level of assurance and confidence that he was able to impart."

She goes on to add: "He achieved so much not through luck but through hard work – one never realised how deeply he had gone into the field he chose. He was a man far ahead of his times — when people were mocking what he was doing he didn't care. He led a varied and rich life."

In a touching tribute on her Instagram page one remark Leisha made strikes a deep note. She wrote: "You lived a life others can only dream of and achieved in one lifetime what others do in ten."

Recalling her own childhood and the interaction between her two grandparents she observes: "My grandmother was extremely tolerant of his idiosyncrasies and exceedingly proud of his achievements."

Even Leisha has her Dr. Watsa food story – in fact two. "My earliest memories are of us dropping my great-grandmother to Satsang in Matunga every Sunday and then buying *jalebis* from the sweet shop Sandesh," she reminisces. "He would often make ice cream at home for us and was extremely fond of cooking."

She goes on to say: "Later in life, I cooked for him and until I became a decent cook – never even having boiled water before – I must say, he was more than happy to try all my experiments, giving me constructive criticism and honest feedback. By the time we were in lockdown, I had graduated to being a cook he approved of and I managed to make him 90 different things over 90 days, most of which he thoroughly enjoyed – if I do say so myself. I also took up baking in my free time since he had such a sweet tooth and now thoroughly enjoy cooking and baking for the family."

Leisha travelled a lot with her grandparents and hence had a chance to see him at work first hand – she went to Bangkok and Singapore with her grandparents when she was 17 years and also to Kerala, Rajasthan, and Delhi.

"Him being a sexologist was not shocking," she explains. "My friends and professors were, in fact, very admiring of him."

As Leisha grew up and got married and he got older, he invited his granddaughter and her new bridegroom to live with him.

"He was rather set in his ways by the time I shifted in to live with him," remembers Leisha. "There was a lot of resistance to any kind of change – for a long time he was not too happy with me running the house either." She found that he could be stubborn and adamant about the way he wanted things done – and realised that she had a large helping of those qualities too – and no prizes for guessing from where she got those genes!

"Yet, when it came down to it, you could talk to him about anything without ever worrying about being judged," she says, her face softening. "He was far ahead of his time, realistic, pragmatic and blunt to a fault. His logic was simple: things happen, why not accept that and openly address them?"

Leisha recalls with much amusement the time when her then husband-to-be met Dr. Watsa, who was only too keen to vet him.

"He naturally had many questions for his granddaughter's fiancé," she recalls. "But all Dean could focus on was the pile of drawings with *Kamasutra* poses stacked on a table next to him. This was of course just one of many things we encountered having lived with him for almost seven years. I once came home to a plastic model of a vagina on our coffee table! On being questioned he very nonchalantly stated he was explaining things to a patient."

Perhaps his most endearing quality, one which exemplified his youthful zest for life was his love for partying even in his later years. "He continued to party even in his '90s, and he loved inviting people home and entertaining them," says Leisha. "When Dean and I went out of town, he would promptly throw a party. Sometimes he would just take off without letting us know where he was going and return very late. It would be very worrying."

During the years that the young couple lived with Dr. Watsa, they witnessed a stream of people come and go. "We've had celebrities and fisherfolk alike breeze through our home over the years," she says. "He always treated everyone the same. Multiple cups of tea and plates of biscuits were handed out every day. Phone calls were answered at 3 am! And we were left puzzled as to what emergency would necessitate a frantic call to your sexologist at that hour!"

But, needless to say, Dr. Watsa would answer every call. "He worked very hard and he saw his work as service to society," explains Leisha. The height of his idealism, she adds, was his exhorting her not to charge her patients. "Work as a volunteer and see it as a service to society; we are privileged, we must give back," he would often tell her. Needless to say, as a young professional just starting a family, she could hardly follow the advice.

"Life with Dada was never dull," Leisha says. "The house now seems so quiet and lifeless. The silence I often longed for is now deafening.

He was and will always remain a person most extraordinary and I'm so proud to be his granddaughter."

Soon after Dr. Watsa passed away, Dean, her husband posted a heartfelt tribute on his Instagram page too: "It's amazing to see the love that the world has shared with Dada (Dr. Watsa). From being the star attraction at our wedding, to celebrities wanting to meet you, to being incredibly funny when you least expected it and to changing India's views on sex. You are truly REMARKABLE!! You will be missed. Keep Heaven in splits. We love you."

Even little Mikhail, who was all of three plus years when his great-grandfather passed away, had his own way of dealing with the loss. "My Dada has gone to heaven," he would say to his Nanima, Deepa. "He has left his mobile here for me to call him in heaven." When she asked him if Dada had left his mobile at home, how could they call him as he had no mobile in heaven, he thought for a few seconds and then promptly said: "Dada has got a new mobile in heaven."

In a poignant representation of the circle of life – which is actually a spiral as the circle doesn't close, just moves to the next stage – little Mikhail had a special ritual every morning and night in the last week before his great grandfather passed on. Deepa narrates: "Mikhail would say, 'Dada, open your mouth, I have to give you your medicines'. Then, Dad would open his mouth and Mikhail would put the tablets into his mouth. The next thing was 'Dada, open your mouth, I want to see if you have swallowed your tablets'. If Dad was still holding them in his mouth, Mikhail would say, 'Dada, swallow, come on swallow, you have to get well'." Thus was the manner in which the youngest member of his family nursed him in his last days.

"I am grateful for the fact that I spent the last six weeks of Dad's life looking after and caring for him, cooking him food that he said he would like to eat and just being with him right through," says Gautam sombrely. "Having been so independent all his life, during the last couple of weeks when he needed support to get off the bed or get up from his chair, he would not want to ask for help. We would constantly argue over this and then half an hour later, we would have a drink together."

Those last weeks when Gautam went and actually lived with his father so that he could care for him, served as a time of renewal and regeneration – of bonds, affection and respect.

"We always knew he had left a very large footprint with all the amazing work he had done and continued to do till the very end," Gautam states. "What we didn't know is just how large that footprint is that he has left behind. We were truly overwhelmed with all the press coverage, phone calls, condolence messages, letters, emails etc. that we have received from people across the world after his passing. It gives me great pride to say my father was a legend."

SOMETHING FOR EVERYONE - 2

Continuing the excerpts from It's Normal!. *Reproduced below are two bits – one with reference to the very young and one concerning older persons.*

SEXUAL ABUSE

A parent must warn the child about sexual abuse. It's not enough to caution him/her about getting into cars and accepting sweets from strangers. Studies show that 90 per cent of molesters - including family members, old retainers and neighbours - are known to and trusted by the children they abuse. Age and sex is no bar.

A parent must refer to the organs that are covered by briefs or a bathing costume as private parts and stress these three points with love and seriousness.

1. No one should touch your private parts.
2. No one should make you touch their private parts.
3. If someone asks you to do either of these things, it is never a secret that you have to keep. Tell mummy or daddy, even if you have promised not to or have been told that something awful will happen if you do. This is a bad secret.

By the time the child is four, he or she should know these rules which should be repeated until they become second nature.

If a parent makes a child comfortable while talking about sex by encouraging questions and observations from the very beginning, it becomes easier to discuss deeper issues as he/she grows up. And he/she will continue to turn to her for interpretation of experiences and ideas. This is how the groundwork for trust and meaningful communication is laid.

QUESTIONS

Q *My girlfriend told me that when she was six years old, a friend of the family forced her to have sex and continued to abuse her for more than a year. I am feeling upset. Can it disturb my love for her?*

A It can be disturbing to discover that your partner was sexually abused as a child. Sometimes finding out about it can make you feel even worse than your partner who has had to live with the knowledge. Sometimes, however, it is a relief to find out that any sexual problems you two might have are not your fault. And understanding where they stem from can help you deal with them. Some people feel rage against the abusers. Some blame their abused partners for having 'allowed' the abuse to happen or, if their sex life together is difficult, feel that their partners let the abusers have the sexual contact which is now denied to them. These feelings are unreasonable, however natural. Counselling can help you be realistic about what happened and also help you both deal with the issues that have been raised. The most helpful attitude is loving sympathy. Patience in your sex life is also important. Knowing about the abuse might explain why your partner does not like certain aspects of sex, and respecting that is important.

Q *I am a thirty-five-year-old man. I am happily married and enjoy a good sex life. My wife and I enjoy being in the nude. Both of us believe in body culture and don't*

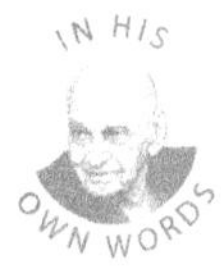

wear clothes while at home. My daughter is seven years old. Is it harmful if parents stay in the nude in front of their children? My child is now comfortable staying in the nude like us. Can we continue to enjoy family nudism? Please advise.

A This is a question often debated in medical circles. Obviously both of you are comfortable with your lifestyle but are you also able to answer your daughter's curious questions? My personal opinion would be to have a minimal cover most of the time. However, this is worthy of debate among readers and they could write in.

Q *My husband and I are worried at the behaviour of our three-year-old who has started playing with his genitals, even in front of guests. How shall we make him understand that he should not do this?*

A As parents you need not be alarmed as genital play among children occurs in the best of homes. No drastic measures are needed - just handle the matter casually and divert the child's attention. When the child is around six years old or more, you may without humiliating, threatening or punishing and at a suitable opportunity, tell the child that such behaviour will not be acceptable. Appealing to the child's pride and sense of responsibility may be all that needs to be done. If the child persists, then take him to a child psychologist.

SEX AT FORTY AND BEYOND

WOMEN

Statistics show that a woman's lifespan is seven years longer than that of a man. With new-age tricks, trends and treats you can look as young as you feel, with your libido well in place. You know, or should know what you want, be it about orgasms, the G-spot or being responsible for your own pleasure.

Even though vaginal lubrication may decrease, you develop an influx system of veins in the genital area around the age of forty, the better to heighten orgasmic response.

Think of menopause (average age fifty-two) as the beginning of a new phase - freedom from menstruation, pregnancy and childbearing. The nasty initial symptoms - sweating, hot flushes, dizziness, headaches, mood swings - can be shortlisted and are treatable. As for vaginal dryness, a lubrication tube is a woman's best friend.

Some women, and may their tribe decrease, kiss sex goodbye because of inhibitions, poor body image, ill health and misconceptions.

Regular sex is what keeps your hormonal balance ticking and increases your erotic appetite. 'I think that people are conned into believing that sexual desire decreases with age. My best sex experiences have come now,' reveals Vinita (ed: name changed), aged fifty-eight.

If women remain sexually active, the changes accompanying menopause are less marked.

MEN

Between forty-five and fifty-five, a man's gonads become less productive; testosterone drops slowly, testicles shrink, erections are not as strong or subside suddenly or take longer to occur. This waning libido and slowing of response is called andropause. And together with worries about career and finances, excess weight, diabetes, boredom with your partner, that can be a noxious brew. Heavy drinking and smoking target the nervous systems and dampen the libido. After forty, every

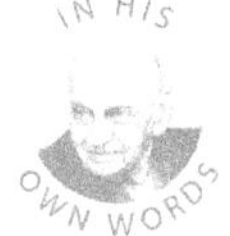

man in the world undergoes some changes. The erections are never as firm as they were two years ago; the penis requires manual handling, preferably by the partner and takes longer to get erect. Embarrassingly, during foreplay or intercourse, the penis may subside suddenly, the spurting action of ejaculation decreases and, with time, semen may just trickle out. At times there may be no ejaculation (no need for anxiety as sex power continues), the quantity and colour of the semen may change and sexual desire may decrease.

Fear of performance creates a vicious cycle – even a single failure seems bad enough to make you want to withdraw from sex altogether. This may distress your partner and leave her wondering about her own attractiveness and whether you have found someone else. Sometimes, the cause of male dysfunction can also be the female as she loses interest in sex.

The good news is, there is help to ensure that no man suffers from erectile dysfunction. Ask a sexologist about allopathic and other alternative medicines and vacuum devices. One of the factors in a midlife crisis is that both partners may be having routine sex with the same person year after year. Some begin to view their mate as a friend, and a sexless person. The partnership then becomes friendly not passionate.

Remember that slower responses can mean longer foreplay and prolonged stimulation can enhance intimacy.

QUESTIONS

Q *My wife is forty years old. Will her sex drive taper off in middle age?*

A It's just the opposite. The female sex drive usually grows stronger when women are free from the fear of pregnancy, childbearing problems and the insecurities of youth. The middle-aged woman who enjoys being herself, delights in exploring her sexuality and has a loving, pleasing partner, should be having the time of her life erotically and emotionally.

Q *I am forty-two years old and have been married for the last six years. We have been unable to have a child. My wife's periods have been irregular since the time we got married. Medication hasn't helped. I have no knowledge of her menstrual cycles. How do I find out whether she really has her periods or not? What if she is fooling me? I am very confused.*

A Firstly, do not lose trust. I am sure she is equally concerned. If you want to take serious action, please accompany her to the doctor, clarify your doubts and understand what should be done. Your sperm count and motility, the frequency of intercourse and your wife's reproductive status need to be investigated.

Q *I am forty-seven years old and married for many years. Though I have led a happy married life so far, of late I have lost interest in my wife. I simply fail to get an erection. Though I do get one on watching others, I haven't been able to satisfy either her or myself. I have tried a homeopathic drug to boost my libido, but now my sperm count is low and I ejaculate just after penetration. What could the problem be?*

A Your roving eyes are playing tricks on you. Take more interest in your wife. I suggest you engage in more foreplay, like a massage or a bath together to arouse your interest. Get a prostate check from a urologist and if you still cannot succeed: Consult a sexologist.

Q *I am a fifty-three-year-old married woman and my menstrual cycle stopped when I was fifty. However, my sex drive is very high, and my husband and I have sex twice a week. Our foreplay and intercourse last about half an hour and I have an orgasm at least three times during the act. I was wondering up to which age one can enjoy sex this way and up to what age I will continue to get orgasms. I do not have any medical problems so far and work out for about two hours a day. My husband too is very active and healthy. Kindly advise.*

A Congrats for being an example to others and I am happy that you are in a state of bliss. You can continue to be so for as long as you desire.

AFTERWORD

TRIBUTES BY FAMILY AND FRIENDS

Edited excerpts from a small selection of the tributes that poured in after the passing of Dr. Mahinder C. Watsa

My Soul Superstar

Dipa De Motwane

Minny Uncle had many avatars for countless people – paterfamilias, friend, mentor, sexpert, a compassionate shoulder, a non-judgmental listener, a trusted confidant. Added to all these attributes, I personally looked up to him as my Soul Superstar.

There was no problem too small or too big for which he didn't have an out-of-the-box solution. I remember venting to him about something that must have been quite inconsequential one day and the twinkle in his eye when he responded – "That was how you felt yesterday, what about today?" That single remark turned my upside down world upright in one simple instant.

He was the guide I trusted most, because his advice was always wise, impartial and practical.

Minny Uncle I miss you. And truly, the universe broke the mould after you.

Amazing, Gentle & Caring

Kamini Khanna

Oh how he loved my mother's *ma ki daal*, Peshawari chicken, or for that matter anything she cooked, as she was an amazing cook! I remember her saying "Minny *yeh kabab khaao khaas aapke liye banaaye hain*". Of course you didn't really have to twist his arm!!

A very practical man, you could tell from his column.

He was my gynaecologist – the only one I could trust. An amazing, gentle, caring doctor and human being – they just don't make them like him anymore.

Family Friends Over Generations

Zinnia Mehta Khajotia

It has been a delightful, three-generational family friendship which continues till today!

Minny Uncle was a doctor at JJ hospital in Bombay and my dad was a medical representative for Johnson & Johnson. Soon, a friendship developed between them and extended to the other family members including the indomitable matriarch, Dadima Bhagwant Kaur, middle brother Jiti and his wife, Kiki. As also their pretty, youngest sister Sheila.

He was a very busy and much sought-after doctor. Reading about him and his work was a source of constant pride to me.

Rest in Peace, Dear Doctor! You certainly brought the prudish Indian out of the closet and emboldened him or her to ask pertinent questions, thereby assuring yourself iconic status! Way to go!

Calming Demeanour, Insightful Knowledge

Yasmin Patel

Dr. Watsa was an institution in Mumbai or dare I say India? It is a daunting idea to pen a few thoughts on Dr. Watsa or just Watsie as he was fondly referred to in our home.

His daily column was different things to different people: for those from a very conservative background, it was a forum where they were given a straight, down to earth answer; to others, his quick wit was a joy to read in answer to some really absurd questions.

He loved sweet dishes and could demolish servings of *kheer* and *shirkurma* with relish at our place.

He always had a calming demeanour and deep and insightful knowledge of medicine. He saved my mother's life when he visited her in a nursing home and prevailed on the staff there to stop a medicine she was highly allergic to... later, he found out that one more dose of it would have been fatal!!

May you rest in peace Dr. Watsa!

A Person Admired by Many

Sister Anne John RJM

I had great regard for Dr. Watsa; he was a person admired by many. I came in contact with him, when he was in charge of the International Planned Parenthood Federation (IPPF). He happened to come in contact with our team, to plan out a teachers training programme on HIV/AIDS.

Once I was asked by Dr. Watsa, "Sr. Anne, How do you manage to carry on all this work?" The answer I gave was this: "I too do not know how." One thing I am sure of is that God is with me and it is He who strengthens me and guides me, to never say "No" to any help required by the poor and needy. And always, my prayer is "Lord I do not ask for an easy life but make me a strong person."

May the good God bless Dr. Watsa and may his soul Rest in Peace. United always in love and prayers.

A Giant Among Men

Bubbli Advani

Minny Uncle you were a constant in the lives of us kids growing up – kind, caring, full of humility and pure in heart and soul. Your calm, practical and reassuring presence always radiated and touched us, making us feel calmer about any difficult situation that arose.

I will never forget attending a wedding with Minny Uncle, Promila Masi and Gautam in a community of fisherfolk in Chimbai, Bandra. Minny Uncle was the Guest of Honour and we could not help but feel the reverence that the villagers felt for him. We were treated like royalty as we walked the streets in a procession with the wedding party.

This is one example of the many lives and communities that Minny Uncle touched. There is a myriad of other such events and stories that relate to his generous character.

A life well lived by a gentle, tall, fair and handsome man. Rest well Uncle – Minny by name but a giant amongst men!

Guide, Friend & Mentor

Yogi Motwane

Minny Jijaji was an amazing guy, because he had this knack of levelling with all – young and old alike. He was a loving, caring, positive personality. I don't recall him having anything negative to say about anyone, friend or foe.

He was a guide, friend and mentor to the extended family and I guess to his patients and the millions of readers who followed his daily column, subtly educating them, in his own way, in something he believed in and at the risk of upsetting some or maybe many. He will be missed.

What I remember most was his passion for food. I often had the pleasure of indulging with him, from a fishing village in the boonies, where he was invited by a patient who was treated for free, to dingy places he had wanted to try and starred restaurants and clubs. He loved his ice cream and desserts.

He would religiously call Bula (my wife) on January 31 every year to wish her a Happy Birthday which she shared with Prom.

Prom now has her *Janaab* back with her.

A Full Life

Muktesh Sharma

Minny Bhai was one you got fond of naturally. Just the thought of him brings a smile to my face. I have had many a long conversation with him. He was soft spoken, uninhibited, non-judgemental, refreshingly frank and with a keen sense of humour. He led a full life and accomplished much, both as a professional and as a family man.

I will miss him greatly.

Understanding the Unspoken

Deepika Motwane

As a child I grew up in a joint family with many uncles and aunts. Minny Uncle was one of them, to whom I would be taken to, for minor ailments like fever, sore throat etc. Under normal circumstances there was always a foreboding dread of seeing a doctor. But going to Minny Uncle was comforting. He was funny, endearing and somehow just 'got you', understanding the unspoken.

Cut to adulthood, I would discuss many cases on a professional level concerning couples' counseling.

His perception and guidance on many levels were astounding. What impacted me most were his insights on female sexuality which unfortunately have not merely been grievously ignored, but cruelly tabooed in our society.

It was a privilege to know him – he shall be remembered both as an uncle and later, as a benevolent mentor.

Progressive Views

Namita Devidayal

I had the privilege of knowing Minny Uncle as an in-law, a journalist's guide and, above all, as a friend.

I shall always cherish his warmth and his progressive views on subjects that few had the guts to discuss.

Once a year, we would meet for lunch at the Willingdon Club or in his sea-dappled home and he would regale me with stories about his work and cases which inevitably left me feeling awestruck, over his clinical objectivity and his compassion!

He has left behind him a remarkable legacy – and definitely many happier bedrooms.

He Impacted Lives

Wg Cdr Rakesh Sharma AC (Retd)

He always was my Minnybhai and so, Promila became my bhabhi. They married when I was about four years old and I was there when it happened! As per Punjabi wedding ritual, the youngest in the family was appointed as the '*sarbala*' and, as the latest entrant to the family, I got a seat on the spotless white mare with Minnybhai astride, as the *baraat* set course for Promilabhabhi's place.

That was then.

Over these years, I have known him as an accomplished medical professional, an empathic listener with a sharp observant mind but, above all, what was clearly evident was his unflappable nature and his zen-like approach towards situations that would make lesser mortals overreact! He hid these traits under a blanket of humour with tongue firmly held in cheek!

Later, as India's leading sexologist he succeeded in breaking down the reserve of many who were in need of his wise counsel. In so doing, he impacted many lives that otherwise would have remained anxious, beset with self doubts or otherwise remained unfulfilled.

Again, as a true Punjabi, he was an unabashed foodie. Many an evening he would call me after leaving his clinic in Bandra; and then would go missing for an hour before turning up at the doorstep laden with brown paper bags stuffed with goodies like samosas, pakoras, jalebis et al. Noticing the furrows deepening on Promilabhabhi's forehead, he would enter his zen state. At times like these, he knew that while speech may be silver, silence was golden!

Oh yes, they were a happy couple and I shall always miss both of them, dearly.

The Economist Pays Homage

After his passing, The Economist *published an article on Dr. Watsa and Katharine Whitehorn in their January 23rd, 2021, edition of the magazine comparing the two pre-eminent British and Indian dispensers of common sense.*

Both columnists continued to a great age, Katherine till 92, Dr. Watsa till almost 97. To quote the article in The Economist:

"Wisdom seemed to gather around them until both were national treasures. Their essential optimism was tempered: Dr. Watsa's by the beatings, abuse and unhappily arranged marriages, he was told of, and could do nothing about; Ms. Whitehorn's by the feeling that sex had come to tyrannise relationships. But the numbers of people they had braced with confidence were legion, and occasionally their advice was similar. To a woman worried about not being a virgin on her wedding night, Dr. Watsa wrote: "Don't worry, your husband won't notice." While to a young bedsitter hostess, cooking for a man, Ms. Whitehorn breezed "Don't apologise, and NEVER ask 'Is It alright?'"

A Jolly Good Person

J.E. Mistry

Dr. Watsa always said FPAI was very close to his heart and he and FPAI could not be separated.

He was a jolly good person – a straightforward man who never indulged in politics or politicking.

We were a two-man team in FPAI when he was the National President and I was the Secretary General from 2003 to 2008.

His knowledge and ability were par excellence where his favourite subject was concerned – adolescence. This was one of the "A's" in the curriculum of FPAI. Dr. Watsa not only wrote quite a lot on this theme, but he fought very much to see that the State Government introduced sexuality education in High Schools.

He not only steered the Mumbai Branch of FPAI during difficult times, but he had also made his presence felt in most of the 40 branches of the organisation spread all over India, and helped them to surmount their problems. He was one who would always see that differences were settled amicably.

Such a man should have been a Patron in the annals of FPAI, but destiny ruled otherwise. Even up to the last year of his life, I took up his cause, because I believed Dr. Watsa was not only a Patron but a Patriarch of FPAI.

An Iconic Sexuality Educator

Vaishali Sinha

I got to know Dr. Mahinder Watsa through the course of making my documentary film *Ask the Sexpert*. The film features his popularity and work as a sex advice columnist, against the backdrop of a ban on sex education curriculums in schools in a third of the country.

There was never a dull moment during our shoots! When I arrived at his home office for our first meeting in 2013, my jaw almost dropped; so shocked was I by his age – 89 then. But of course, I was charmed by his stylish ways. How amazing, at that age, to be able to connect with such a wide variety of readers of his column – or, as he was fond of saying, "vibe with them".

Upon the film winning an award at a festival in Washington DC, the organiser Mr. Manoj Singh wrote to me suggesting a petition for a national honour and award for him. His words: "Dr. Watsa must be recognised by the government and should be awarded a Padma Shri or a Padma Bhushan. Please write to the PM's and President's Offices, we will do the same."

Dr. Watsa's response in his typical understated manner was – I have already received a Life-time Achievement Award (he had been so recognised by both the World Association of Sexologists and at the Asia Pacific Congress of Sexology 2004).

After an online screening of the film at the South Asian Feminist Film Festival organised by Kriti Film Club and Sangat, I came across a post on social media by the pioneering feminist and founder of Sangat, the late Kamala Bhasin calling him a "beautiful young man".

Kindness & Tolerance

Rivca Elias

Though I had met Dr. Watsa only twice, I had read his column every day in the *Mumbai Mirror* and all the sad, sometimes funny, questions that the readers mailed to him for his expert advice.

I come from a family of medical doctors since the time of my grandmother. Yet, this family of doctors was mentally rooted in the Jane Austen era where sex and relationships were concerned.

When I started reading Dr. Watsa's column, I realised that here was a man who was totally free of any inhibitions in explaining things to the clueless public and also that there was a kindness and a tolerant understanding in him of people who did not have that knowledge or were too inhibited to ask or to find out for themselves.

When I was in my teens, there was no talk of women having any desires whatsoever. Dr. Watsa changed all that.

Connecting Across Generations

Prakash Bhalerao

Dr. Watsa imparted education on the taboo subject of sex in a most witty manner. Sometimes he cajoled, sometimes whispered and at times blew cool, soothing air on the oozing wound, and offered great comfort.

My only regret is I did not get to steal even one evening out of his life! I was very sorry to read that this "Watsayana" of India's modern sexology is no more.

What always also amazed me in his writing was his way in approaching the subject which seamlessly crossed generational boundaries. This is the most difficult feat for a writer to achieve.

Writing Without Hypocrisy

An Ardent Admirer

Let me confess, I was an ardent reader of the *Times of India*, attributable to the fact that it carried this sensation called the *Mumbai Mirror*. From the *TOI* bunch the first thing I did was to prune out the *Mumbai Mirror* and flip through its pages, and only then did I go through the pages of the mainstream *TOI*.

The brightest spark of the *Mumbai Mirror* was the Sexpert section by Dr. Mahinder Watsa. Being a man and a bachelor, with no wife to frown at me while this naughty column absorbed the whole of me, I truly relished the humour and the uncanny traits of Dr. Watsa. It was neither full of jargon nor did it carry mundane technicalities; yet it is a non-hyprocritical writing that drives a sensitive message in the most candid, hilarious manner.

Not One to Wear His Accolades on His Sleeve

Nina Puri

In an area where tradition and misplaced morality, especially in India can't, or does not, meet reality, Dr. Watsa furrowed a pioneering and difficult path – on the subject of sex and sexuality, where even angels fear to tread – well over four-and-a-half decades ago.

Dr. Watsa, after his innings as a gynaecologist and obstetrician, had worked with Glaxo Laboratories, and often shared his experiences of that time with us in FPAI. Shifting gears decades later, he remained fully engaged as a Consultant in the area of Reproductive Health and Sexuality, cognizant of the lack of awareness in matters of sexual behaviour, knowledge and understanding amongst couples and young boys and girls. In 1974, on Dr. Watsa's advice and suggestion, FPAI launched Sex Education, Counseling and Therapy Centres (SECRT), and also initiated a Young Inspirers Group.

Dr. Watsa had a long, successful, impactful and meaningful innings during which he often left clients stumped through his googlies. Appreciation, awards and distinctions sat lightly on his shoulders – though he had many, he never wore them on his sleeve!

All of us have to pass on, but some like Dr. Watsa, leave a distinct fragrance and aroma, and a legacy to match. In his body of work he managed to change manifold times troubled individual lives into bliss and happiness in personal relationships, especially young people.

Radiating Warmth & Affection

Mohan Shahani

My association with Dr. Mahinder Watsa goes back several decades. More than 70 years back my sister Susheila, who was about his age used to mention the names of two smart and charming boys, namely Rajin and Minny.

Then a few years later, my dear wife Dr. Shanti was doing her internship at Navrozji Wadia Hospital, in the ObGyn field where Minny was a senior Resident.

Later, Minny joined Glaxo Laboratories, where he was in charge of Marketing; and my sister Susheila, a microbiologist, was a production supervisor.

Thereafter, Shanti and I used to meet Minny and his charming wife Promila (Prom) socially.

We had a large number of common friends; and we all had many decades of a happy relationship together. Those were wonderful times with countless parties and holiday travels. Our strong bonds have continued with the younger generation.

Parties hosted by Minny and Prom used to be quite entertaining, sometimes with some new ideas! And this was quite characteristic of Minny! To have a new, innovative activity instead of a routine formal sort of party.

Dr. Minny Watsa was a very good human being. A great man and a very good friend. He radiated warmth and affection. His winning smile is a joyful legacy to be cherished by us for evermore.

An Inspiring Leader with a Golden Heart

Nandini Johri

I had known Dr. Mahinder C. Watsa since January 1986, and got immense opportunities to gain knowledge and skills from him.

At my first meeting with Dr. Watsa at a workshop in Devlali, I found that all participants were amazed by his radiant personality and wisdom.

Dr. Watsa was very fond of Young Inspirers, which we formed in Lucknow, and he ensured that the enthusiasm of these young volunteers was sustained and they received ample opportunities to enhance their skills and gain further knowledge. Later, SECRT Rajkot and Jabalpur branches also formed Young Inspirers groups.

Dr. Watsa was and will always remain my Mentor, Guide, Guru,

Guardian… He will continue to live with us forever through the ripple effect of his teachings, trainings and guidance and, I am sure, even now he is blessing us from his heavenly abode along with Ma'am, Mrs. Promila Watsa.

Mahinder as a toddler

The Wats brothers as young boys (fm l) Jitender, Rajinder and Mahinder

A young Mahinder looking ahead with dreams in his eyes

Grant Medical College Football XI (1946-1947): M.C. Watsa (Vice-captain) seen seated (2nd fm l)

Starting out on a promising career – both earnest seriousness and humour firmly on board

With the members of B.Y. L. Nair Charitable Hospital, Gynaecology & Obstetrics Ward (1950): Dr. M.C. Watsa, M.B.B.S. (Houseman) seated (ext r)

Mahinder weds Promila

Dr. Watsa on his way to the UK

A young Promila

Mahinder and Promila enjoying a romantic moment in the UK

Promila with son Gautam – smiling brightly

The world in his arms – Dr. Watsa with Promila and Gautam

Dr. Watsa and Promila with Rajin and Savitri in December 1962

Dr. Watsa (centre with tie) during his time at Glaxo checking on the workings of the packaging department

Dr. Watsa and Promila after being felicitated at the Glaxo farewell for him

With Patricia Schiller and Mr. Schiller

Dr. Watsa seen with CSEPI colleagues Dr B. K. Mahipal (ctr) and Dr. Vithal Prabhu (r)

Dr. Watsa at a cultural evening during an event in the Philippines in the late 1980s

Dr. Watsa during his visit to Canberra, Australia in 1990 where he was a speaker at the World Congress on AIDS

Dr. Watsa (centre row, 2nd fm l) with the delegates at the Workshop on Leadership and Management Development for Reproductive Health Services in India

Dr. Watsa speaking at a CSEPI conference

Dr. Watsa at the Golden Jubilee Celebration of IMA C. L. Jhaveri Oration (11-03-1984)

Dr. Watsa speaking at the 1st National Conference of IASECT

At the International Conference on 'Men as Partners in Reproductive Health'

The compound and cottage that housed Dr. Watsa's original Bandra clinic

Dr. Watsa at his new Bandra clinic

With Nurse May (2nd fm r) and members of her family in October 2008

Dr. Watsa enjoying a light moment on the sidelines of a meeting

Dr. Watsa with Nandini Johri at Singapore airport in 1995

Promila admiring the trophy: At a function where Dr. Watsa received the Lifetime Achievement Award during the Asia Pacific Congress

Dr. Watsa and Promila look on as their son Gautam weds Deepa

Dr. Watsa dancing at his son's wedding

Dr. Watsa with Devi Vaswani (Deepa's mother)

Dr. Watsa, Promila and Gautam (standing) at dinner with Promila's younger brother Kiran

Deepa with Dr. Watsa and Promila

Dr. Watsa sharing a joyful moment with baby Ayesha

Dr. Watsa with a young Leisha

Promila with close friends Sudha Kini and Vasant Kamte at a party in 2003

Dr. Watsa and Promila – an enduring loving and supportive relationship

Promila and Dr. Watsa celebrating their 50th wedding anniversary

Dr. Watsa and Promila with the entire family – (fm l) Deepa, Leisha, Gautam and Ayesha on the occasion of their 50th wedding anniversary celebration

Dr. Watsa at Leisha and Dean's wedding with the bridal couple

Dr. Watsa holding the V. V. Poorie Award

Dr. Watsa flanked by son Gautam, and Leisha carrying baby Mikhail

Seeing life through a humorous lens – at one of his birthday parties, sporting a tie presented to him by his family as a joke

The eternal foodie – Enjoying a falooda at the club!

On Dr. Watsa's 94th birthday: with great-grandson Mikhail on his lap, Leisha (standing ext r) and colleagues and friends

Dr. Watsa with Ashok Row Kavi

Dr. Watsa with Dr. Russi Baam and Dr. Ruby Baam at one of his birthday celebrations

Dr. Watsa with long-time friend Dr. Palarp Sinhaseni (on l) at a conference

Four generations of the Watsa family: (fm l) Dr. Watsa, Leisha, Gautam with little Mikhail

Nilan Singh, a Mumbai-based media professional, has enjoyed a career arcing over journalism, television and corporate communications, spanning several decades.

Over the years, she has held senior editorial positions in established general interest, lifestyle and business publications, such as *Sunday Observer, Savvy, Gentleman,* amongst others. She has been involved in various capacities, including content creation and as producer and co-producer for TV projects for broadcasters *Zee TV, BBC's Channel Four* etc.

Nilan also set up a corporate communications agency that has handled a range of key assignments for national and international clients.

Known for her meticulous research and her engaging style of writing, Nilan has now authored her first book.

www.ingramcontent.com/pod-product-compliance
Lightning Source LLC
LaVergne TN
LVHW010544160826
845677LV00013B/2994

* 9 7 9 8 8 8 9 3 5 8 2 9 9 *